THORNSBY BY FRED MCLAREN

The Complete Comic Collection

THORNSBY BY FRED McLAREN

The Complete Comic Collection

Tom McLaren

and

Mary McLaren

Next Chapter

PUBLISHING

LOS ANGELES, CALIFORNIA

Manufactured in the United States of America

10 9 8 7 6 5 4 3 2 1

ISBN 978-1-7356215-2-4 [deluxe hardcover]

ISBN 978-1-7356215-0-0 [hardcover] / ISBN 978-1-7356215-1-7 [softcover]

Library of Congress Control Number 2020919616

First Edition: September 2020

A DIVISION OF NEXT CHAPTER ENTERTAINMENT LLC

For Fred McLaren

A snapshot of his immense talent is captured on these pages. Thornsby impacted more people than he realized. He would have been very proud to see this book reach publication.

Fred McLaren. Chicago, Illinois. 1960s.

THORNSBY by FRED McLAREN
The Complete Comic Collection

Contents

Fred McLaren with his sons Tom (left) and Fred. New Lenox, Illinois. 1960s.

Introduction

by Tom McLaren

My Memories From the Thornsby Years

Some childhood memories remain vivid despite the passage of time, bringing with them an unmistakable and somewhat indescribable sentimental quality. The happy ones that stimulated our senses in the past often become melancholy aches over time. We yearn to go back in time, just to relive those precious moments. As children, the world seemed infinite and we never thought to soak in those fleeting moments. As adults, we remember through rose-colored glasses the feelings and the mood more than the details. If only we could go back in time and wrap ourselves once again in that soft and warm blanket of contentment.

The first 12 years of my life were spent in the tiny town of New Lenox, Illinois - a suburb southwest of Chicago. When I was born, dad Homer Frederick McLaren (who went simply by 'Fred' in his adult years), mom Betty Lou, and older brother Frederick Robert (yes, a second 'Fred' in our small family) moved into a small suburban house in this quiet farming community. New Lenox at that time was surrounded by corn fields as far as the eye could see and had a population of approximately 1,000 (not counting cattle). These were truly the white picket fence years for all of us, with dad commuting on the Rock Island Line train into the big city of Chicago for his creative art director day job, mom staying home and happily caring for the house and all three 'boys' within, and my brother and I playing in our backyard (it seemed so large through a child's eyes), which bordered a small trickling stream named Hickory Creek. Wiffle ball, fishing, and catching fireflies (we called them lightning bugs in those days) were the off school pastimes - and we even had our own swing in the backyard built on a frame of old telephone pole logs.

It was a single story house, but a second level housed a large unfinished attic and one small adjacent room which became my father's den and studio. He would retreat there every night immediately after dinner, to work on his freelance art and writing projects. It was his private space for leisure time as well (he was never the typical dad watching TV in the living room with the family; in fact, TV viewing was dissuaded after dinner so the noise would not bother him). In the evenings, my mother would read romance novels on the living room couch and my brother and I would play in our separate bedrooms. There were exceptions on Monday nights when the family would all sit down to watch "Laugh-In" during its initial years (my dad appreciated the irreverent humor) and on late Saturday nights when we'd watch "Creature

Features" (reruns of the old classic Universal monster movies) on WGN.

To reach his second story den, we had to walk through the master bedroom and approach what appeared to be a closet door. It opened to reveal a hidden staircase, which led upstairs to this small room, which was separated from the rustic attic by a wooden door. This is where my vivid memory begins . . .

As a small boy, I would sit at the bottom of these stairs in the darkness. The slick cold wood steps would creak under normal weight, so I would sit quietly at the bottom of the stairs and listen to the sounds coming from dad's studio - usually the radio playing a Chicago Cubs game or an oldies station featuring the big band sounds of Harry James. I would slowly inch my way up the steps one at time (I felt like I was hiding from something, but what? Most likely I knew he was working, so I must be quiet).

When I would make my entrance to this room, it was like stepping into fantasyland. The room was not a typical square shape: it had nooks and odd-shaped corners with a very slanted ceiling reflecting the peak of the roof. In current vernacular, it was a man cave but that description doesn't do it proper justice. Visually, it was filled with all types of print memorabilia: books, magazines, newspapers, and clippings. Art was everywhere, in all forms of media (pencil sketches, watercolor paintings, small sculptures, etc.). A coffee table in an alcove was home to a miniature train set, stacks and rows of paperbacks and digest-sized magazines, and a matted photograph of an artistic female nude. The bookcase was filled with hardcover books including many first editions, with an antique wood pirate ship displayed on the top shelf. It was not a disorganized or messy space, the belongings seemed to fit the room perfectly. I definitely learned my collector mentality from my dad (which is both a blessing and a curse, as I look today at my own overflowing man cave).

The room was built around a sturdy and large wood drawing board, next to a small credenza desk for art supplies, a large coffee mug, and an ashtray. When I was very young I could barely see over this desk, but most memories have me tall enough to see the in-process art project of the moment being detailed on his drawing board. If the radio wasn't playing, there was a large hi-fi record player cabinet (the type with a heavy lid which was lifted up before you placed the vinyl on the spindle) spinning the sounds of Sinatra or a jazzy instrumental. The air was always thick with cigarette smoke. He went through brief cigar and pipe smoking phases, but it was a smoldering cigarette that is a constant in all my memories. I absorbed the sights, sounds and smells of my father's hobbies and interests, but I learned at a very young age to never touch any of his belongings. I honestly don't remember being taught this. It's just how it was: you treat other people's belongings with respect.

I would volunteer to refill his coffee mug, because I loved having a useful task to do. I would trot back down the stairs, go into the kitchen (I learned to make coffee at quite a young age, though curiously I never became a coffee drinker in later life), and then slowly - carefully - carry the steaming cup of java back up to him. I would then usually just stand by the table, watching and absorbing it all. It was fascinating to see him work on his illustrations and cartoons. While most young boys learn about spark plugs and fuel pumps from their father, I instead learned about X-Acto knives, Wite-Out and Zip-A-Tone (a now defunct screentone paper used frequently in the Thornsby cartoons). I knew I was watching talent in action and it was mesmerizing.

Sometimes he would put on a children's record album to keep me entertained for longer periods. Most children's records were very annoying to him, but a small handful were deemed acceptable - Shari Lewis and Lambchop, the Pinocchio movie soundtrack, and one other I so wish I had kept (a story album with train sounds). I would sit in an oversized cushioned chair in a corner of the room, with my feet on the footstool and I would inevitably fall asleep during the record's first side. Other times I would just sit in the chair without the stereo playing and listen to the sounds from outside. The room had no air conditioning, so during the summer months the window next to the drawing board was always open. The window looked into a tall apple tree by the side of the house. It was not uncommon to hear the hoot of an owl and there was always a train whistle in the distance. There was a grassy field on the other side of Hickory Creek which was always deserted (except for an occasional wandering cow). This field bordered the train tracks, so we were actually just one block away from the railroad. This is likely why I feel comforted by the sound of a distant train to this very day.

To bring this story full circle, I remember my dad created Thornsby in this environment. The first year of Thornsby's creation happened in this room at this drawing board. He would often complete the inking on a week's worth of cartoons and then tape them to the wall to dry. My mother would come upstairs to nod approvingly (this is the only time I remember my mom being in his room!). I too would do the museum-style walk and study them one by one. I was too young to completely understand the political humor and too naïve to fully comprehend some of the 1970s socioeconomic issues, but I loved it nonetheless. It was an exciting time for all of us and certainly the peak of dad's entire life.

Fred McLaren in his home den and studio. New Lenox, Illinois. 1973.

Thornsby - Background and History

My father was born on June 24, 1930 in Springfield, Illinois. My grandfather Homer Douglas McLaren was a lawyer and wanted his son to follow in his footsteps. Dad however rebelled from the very start, because he was clearly born to be an artist. His interests and hobbies all revolved around the creative arts. He loved pulp magazines, comic books, Big Little Books, radio shows, and feature films. After high school, he married my mother Betty Lou Spring and temporarily postponed his art career when he was drafted into the Korean War. After returning from Hawaii where he was stationed, they moved to Chicago and he entered the American Academy of Art in 1954 under the tutelage of William Mosby. After three intensive years studying illustration and fine arts, he graduated and began to live his dream.

He worked in all types of media: oil paint, watercolor, pastel, charcoal, pen and ink, etc. A fan and collector of many great artists, he would frequently cite Vernon Grant, Arthur Rackham, N.C. Wyeth, Haddon Sundblom, Milton Caniff, Alberto Vargas, J.C. Leyendecker, and Will Eisner as his many influences. Jack Davis, Frank Frazetta, Alex Nino and Jose Gonzalez were contemporary artists that he admired. He combined his personal love of art with business by finding employment in the commercial art profession. He served as art director for various magazines and also did graphic design and illustration for numerous advertising clients through the 1960s. He always supplemented his day job (one employer during this time was IIT, the Illinois Institute of Technology) with freelance writing and illustration for numerous print publications, including books, in-house publications, and newspaper supplement magazines.

Fred McLaren working on a commercial art project. Chicago, Illinois. 1960s.

14

It was during his early years at the American Academy of Art that his passion for professional cartooning was ignited. He and a friend created and collaborated on a newspaper comic strip titled "Captain Stark." Clearly inspired by his love for "Terry & the Pirates" and other similar newspaper comics, Stark was an adventure strip based under the seas, with a continuing storyline. When this idea failed to find a publisher, he went solo with his second creation in the early 1960s: a single-panel newspaper comic about a group of beatniks. This idea too was greeted with rejection, as is typical in all forms of budding creative and artistic expression. Success needs perseverance.

Throughout the remainder of the 1960s and early 1970s, he focused primarily on commercial art at RR Donnelly & Sons, a large commercial printing company for books, magazines, catalogs, periodicals, and advertising and promotion materials. Certainly the peak of his corporate career, he was art director over many major accounts (a high point was his successful national campaign for Sylvania during 1971-72, both in print and in-store). During this 'Mad Men' advertising era, he did graphic design, wrote copy, and drew illustrations for various ad agencies and other business clients.

He continued to pursue fine art for his personal satisfaction, as well as resale in local galleries. He would take his prized 1955 Morgan sports car on road trip vacations and return with the trunk filled with freshly painted oil and watercolor landscapes. His personal time was always spent sketching a variety of subjects, from portraits of friends to caricatures of strangers. He loved spending time in coffee and donut shops, where he would sketch on napkins or whatever was handy whenever the whim would strike him.

By the early 1970s his desire to be a syndicated newspaper cartoonist and writer moved to the forefront. Out of this fervor came his creation of Thornsby. A very original idea - a single-panel newspaper comic (originally titled "Today's Trauma") with a lead character named Elmer Crabtree. Prior to publication Elmer would be name changed to Thornsby, the perfect moniker for a middle aged everyman living in the 1970s but longing for his nostalgic youth of the 1940s. Thornsby was a family man with an unidentified office job that he didn't enjoy. He lived in a drab suburb named Sludgeville. The world was changing around him and there was nothing he could do to stop it.

Our hero would use his unique sense of humor to deal with all of the decade's culture shocks and current events - from inflation and politics to women's liberation and pollution. His wife Blanch was sympathetic and tolerant of his quirks. His son Tune-In was a free spirited hippie who Thornsby would look at with bewilderment. It was not a family of dysfunctional antagonists. Thornsby would poke fun at his wife and son, as they did in return, but my dad always pointed out they were not "The Bickersons," a radio show from his youth about an argumentative married couple, or "The Lockhorns," a contemporary newspaper comic strip about a quarrelsome couple. The Thornsby family truly cared about each other, but usually with wry amusement over the 1970s situations thrust upon them.

Was Thornsby an autobiographical portrait of Fred McLaren? Physically, they bore no resemblance. You will however see a cartoon version of my father as an unnamed recurring character (usually a friend, business associate, or innocent bystander) in a large number of the panels. Look for the thinner, taller man with combed back hair and eyeglasses and you'll spot him. Personality-wise, I would say nearly all of Thornsby's captions mirrored my dad's opinions and sense of humor. Thornsby's hobbies, interests, and general state of mind are clearly my father's world in the 1970s. For example, it's not a coincidence that Thornsby owned a Morgan sports car and loved the "Inner Sanctum" radio show. Recurring themes of hating Monday mornings, enjoying girlie magazines, and being perplexed by the younger generation were cases of art imitating life. He and Thornsby were both repelled by doctors and dentists (hence, the creation of unsympathetic supporting characters Amorphous Dread, MD and Jimmy Soregums, DDS). He and Thornsby leered at the newly braless generation of young beautiful women (my mother, like Blanch, would roll her eyes and sigh with exasperation at this - which of course made it all the more fun for dad).

Promotional Thornsby cartoon with Fred McLaren looking in the mirror and seeing Thornsby in his reflection.

As I review the cartoons in this book, I see my father in every one of them. There are a few minor exceptions to this rule - for instance, Thornsby was an occasional golfer but my dad never golfed. I also frequently see my mother in Blanch, a happy homemaker who put up with her husband's idiosyncrasies and views. Thornsby's college age son Tune-In was the opposite of me and my brother though (we were grade school and high school kids, respectively, and far too young for the anti-establishment hippie lifestyle). Tune-In and his sexy girlfriend Vibes were definitely inspired by the young adults my dad would encounter in Chicago and later in London, Ontario. An unnamed college age daughter was introduced in the final year to add some variety to the Thornsby family.

My family definitely influenced some of the ideas and captions, but it's all interpreted through my father's eyes. I do realize certain caption references to pop culture ("The Towering Inferno," Ann-Margret, Carpenters, and Grand Funk Railroad to name just a few) were influenced by my interests during those years. But once again I view many of these comics with a bittersweet pang, because it was a much simpler time in my life. Despite all the stresses of everyday living, I see Thornsby muddling through it all with a sense of humor. When I see him happily sitting in his den surrounded by all his toys, I recall my dad in his private room surrounded by his beloved possessions. I see a happy family in these cartoons and I recall the best part of my childhood years.

For historical accuracy, Thornsby was contracted on August 31, 1972 with the National Newspaper Syndicate in Chicago. Newspaper publication started on April 16, 1973 in the St. Louis Post-Dispatch and a handful of other newspapers. Thornsby was picked up in several major cities during its run, including Chicago, Detroit, Philadelphia, Baltimore, and Boston, as well as numerous smaller cities. Thornsby was most popular in the Midwest and on the east coast. My family moved to Canada in August 1973 and my father continued his work by mailing the original artwork to the syndicate's office in Chicago. In total, 768 cartoons were published through September 27, 1975. These three years were my dad's lifelong dream come true and undoubtedly the pinnacle of his professional career. It was a heady time for him, exhilarating and the best of times in many respects.

Fred McLaren working on Thornsby. The specific cartoon on his drawing board was the one published July 21, 1973. New Lenox, Illinois. 1973.

Camelot doesn't last forever as we all know, and by mid-1975 problems with the syndicate caused an early demise for Thornsby. It's a long and complicated story. Suffice to say, I don't remember dad talking much about it, but of course I was young and didn't feel the full impact personally. As with all forms of professional success in entertainment, you never know when something is a once-in-a-lifetime moment until you're old and gray, looking back on a life that's hopefully been well-lived.

Post-Thornsby

My dad had a few other ideas about returning to the newspaper comic world in the years that followed, but I think he was somewhat jaded by the behind-the-scenes business turmoil. His drive to return to cartoon syndication was now weaker. He was always happiest at his drawing board, creating Thornsby in isolation, without the interference of social interaction, business politics, and other factors out of his control. Two comic strip ideas were developed in the mid-70s (during the Thornsby run or shortly afterwards), which yielded a sampling of comics to pitch for syndication. "Gimbol's Girls" was a strip (not a single-panel) about a kindly Grandpa and his two polar opposite granddaughters, one a playmate type named Yummy and the other a staunch feminist named Nails. "Stew & Fret" was a strip about a middle aged man named Stew and his sexy young wife named Fret. Both strips were pitched, but unfortunately rejected. A couple other ideas during the 70s were also planned but never left the pitch stage.

With my brother now in college in London, Ontario, my parents and I returned to the United States in July 1977, settling in Royal Oak, Michigan, a suburb of Detroit. My parents had a turbulent divorce two years later. Dad slowly walked away from the commercial art world during the 1980s. The business was rapidly evolving and he did not embrace the eventual shift to computerized digital work. He embarked on a new life with Chris Ledbetter (she too is an

Fred McLaren, a self-portrait. Chicago, Illinois. 1990s.

artist and designer, and a dear friend to me and my wife Mary), and returned to painting and illustration for one last major burst of creativity.

He briefly toyed with the idea of reviving Thornsby in the early 1980s, but the plan did not come to fruition. I found one piece of original art in his collection referencing Reaganomics and showing a slightly less paunchy Thornsby. It shows what might have been - Thornsby trying to cope with the culture shock of the 1980s. In fact, this concept of Thornsby trying to adapt to each new decade could have survived to this very day. Like Thornsby, my dad grudgingly accepted change and not-so-quietly longed for the good old days.

In the late 1980s dad returned solo to New Lenox and then to Chicago, his favorite city in the world, for the remainder of his life. He found other sources of income, but always continued to do artwork in his spare time. From a business viewpoint, he no longer desired to deal with people who took the joy out of his creative vocation. From a personal viewpoint, he created art to please himself first and foremost. During his retired years, he continued to draw cartoons with humorous captions (once a cartoonist, always a cartoonist!). He would sketch them on notepads, post-its, and scratch pieces of paper. He'd mail them to me and a handful of relatives and friends. I saved every single one of them.

Dad fell ill in 2015 and was hospitalized just prior to Christmas. The doctors discovered he had just weeks left to live. It's times like this when you realize you wish you had said or done various little things during those last few years. At the time I had about 100 Thornsby newspaper clippings digitized and I wanted to make a homemade book to give to him. Mary rushed a book to print and during our last visit, we presented it to him. He was in hospice care and unable to speak, but I could see the recognition in his eyes as I held the book up and said "It's a book of Thornsby." I flipped the pages for him to see the cartoons and told him "Thornsby will live forever." It is my sincere hope, through you, the kind reader who is holding a copy of this book, this statement will come true.

Tom McLaren

August 2020

"THORNSBY"

Chapter 1

Thornsby: Creation & Launch

All artistic projects require extensive planning and bursts of magical creative energy. The evolution of Thornsby from rough outline sketches to the final published output is a fascinating journey. It began with a lead character originally named Elmer Crabtree (and subsequently re-named Thornsby). During the initial months, Fred developed the overall concept, the regular players, and a cast of zany recurring characters. Then the labor starts: a cartoonist/writer needs several weeks of sample comics to convince the decision-makers that the project is sellable, with legs strong enough for a prosperous future.

Pitching the project to various newspaper syndicates is the next step. Fred's original drawings (and the initial three month run) were on large-format 14" x 17" paper. He would carry his bulky professional portfolio case loaded with Thornsby originals into Chicago and work the business side of cartooning. The (now-defunct) National Newspaper Syndicate agreed to carry Thornsby in the summer of 1972. One can argue that now the work truly begins, with a required output of 6 completed single-panel cartoons per week. Over time, Fred would reduce the size of his original drawings to 7" x 8", making the process more manageable and less time-consuming.

Once sold to a syndicate, the marketing machine spreads the word. Glossy paper press books are distributed to newspapers across the country. Triumph comes at last when the comic is picked up for publication and then seen by the newspaper buying audience. Longevity depends on a variety of factors, some of which the cartoonists can control and some of which they cannot. Talent, money, personal tastes, business decisions, fandom, etc. head up a long and complicated recipe for success.

The following pages reveal a behind-the-scenes snapshot of Thornsby's beginnings. Some of these images have only been seen by Fred's eyes until now.

THE PITCH DECK

Thornsby's original nine page pitch deck reveals the major concepts and characters, some of which were retained for the published run, while others were discarded.

The name change of Elmer Crabtree to Thornsby is the most significant post-pitch deck alteration. Other names in the deck such as Tune-In (Thornsby's son), Vibes (Tune-In's girlfriend), and Linda (Dr. Amorphous Dread's nurse) were never actually used in the captions of any published cartoon.

Note also a reference to panels (single-panel comics) and strips (multi-panel sequential comics). This deck was prepared before Fred decided Thornsby would be a Monday-Saturday single-panel comic.

The similarities between Fred and Thornsby are evident from the very start - many of the words in the lower left on the opposite page describe Fred to a T.

"Now Don't get upset dear – maybe he's got a good job! "

In most panels and about ½ of all strips

BLANCA
CRABTREE,
HIS WIFE.
40-45
INTENTIONAL
MISSPELLING.
– IN ON THE
PROBLEM
BUT, WHILE
PUTTING HIM
ON, NEVER
PUTS HIM
DOWN.
A NICE LADY
WITH A SENSE
OF FUN

"Try to understand dear—
He'll never go for Harry
James"

"TUNE-IN"
CRABTREE —
ABOUT 20—
HIS SON.
EVERYTHING
YOU ALWAYS
WANTED TO
KNOW ABOUT
THE COLLEGE
SET AND SOME
YOU COULD
CARE LESS
ABOUT

"VIBBS"

THE
GIRL
FRIEND
AND
ROOMATE
OF
"TUNE-IN"
CRABTREE
—
THE
WHOLE
BRALESS
BIT AND
THE
TERROR
OF ELMER
CRABTREE.
—
A TRAUMA
IN EVERY
PANEL
—
A NICE
KID BUT
"WITH IT"

AMORPHOUS
DREAD
M.D.
— HIS DOCTOR

NO HELP.
NO LOGIC.
AND
NO HOUSECALLS.
—

EVERY
LAYMAN'S
FRUSTRATION
—

HAS "LINDA"
AN ULTRA
SEXY NURSE.

"She stopped my Playboy subscription but I've still got the movie ads."

GRIM JIM –

A NEIGHBOR ADDICTED TO X RATED MOVIES AND LOAFING.

MIDDLE AGED CLUTCHING THE PAST WHILE DENYING IT.

A FOIL TO ELMER'S DISMAY

first appearance – single panel

GORDON DARWIN

HIS BOSS –

HASN'T SMILED IN YEARS.

INSISTS ALL TV COMMERCIALS BE BAD IN ORDER TO BE GOOD

A NAMELESS
DIRTY OLD
MAN
APPEARS—
AS BOOKDEALER,
IN CROWD
SCENES,
IN BACKGROUND
ON STREETS

first
appearance

4 Panel
Strip
—

My Mommy
through out
all my
old comics—

INSTANT
SHRINK—

AN OLD
FRIEND AND
A PSYCHOANALYST.

WITH MULTI
HANG-UPS
AND A MOTHER
FIXATION.
ABOUT AS
MUCH HELP
TO ELMER
AS A
LEAKY
BEDPAN

CONTINUING
CHARACTERS
—

NIXON
MCGOVERN
WALLACE
AGNEW
HOPE
CARSON SHOW
—

SEXPOTS.
PANHANDLERS.
DOOR TO—
DOOR
SALESMEN.
PROTESTORS.
TUNE-IN'S
FRIENDS
—

REACCURING
SUBJECTS
—

POLLUCTION.
THE NEW
POLITICS.
FASHIONS.
MORALS.
PRODUCT FAILURE
GENERATION GAP.
NEW RELIGION.
LIBERATION.
PROTESTS.
PUBLIC OPINION
ADVERTISING.

29

FRED MCLAREN

Born 1930, Springfield, Illinois

Following high school, served with the Army during the Korean War. Entered Chicago's American Academy of Art, September 1954. Studied drawing and painting for three years under William Mosby. Knocked at syndicate doors following art school for five years with a series of both panels and comix strips based on adventure and "beatnik" humor, which were greeted with an immediate lack of response. Pressed into commercial art by economic needs, served on various magazines as an art director and began doing graphic design for advertising and promotion work in the mid-1960's. Cartooning featured in GTE Sylvania's national advertising campaigns in 1971 and 1972, including Sunday newspaper supplements and point of purchase displays. Annual report designs for many national firms including Sears, Roebuck and Company in 1970, 1971 and 1972. Free lance humorous illustrations for books, house organs and Sunday supplements. Feature article writing, 1967-1971, for the Chicago Daily News, Chicago Sun-Times and Chicago Today.

Hobbies include collecting comics, pulp magazines, books and old radio tapes; chess, watercolor painting and restoration of a 1955 +4 Morgan sports car.

Married, two sons, Fred, 16, and Tom, 11. A resident of New Lenox, Illinois since 1961.

Fred's personal biography from 1972, just prior to the launch of Thornsby.

PROMOTIONAL BROCHURE

The National Newspaper Syndicate issued a four page brochure, which folded out to a poster-sized four page reverse, to launch sales to local newspapers.

HOW MANY OF YOUR READERS HAVE A PROBLEM WITH THE SEVENTIES?

THORNSBY

**and his family
and friends all have
the same problem: change**

**but they greet the changes
of the 1970s with warm humor
and a sense of fun!**

"Try to understand, Dear. He'll never go for Harry James."

"Why, it's Mr. Thornsby!"

"Well, it finally happened . . . They recalled everybody's car on the same day."

". . . Signed up for ceramics and basket weaving and have a groovy roommate—38-26-37—so college seems well worth your money . . .

"For your gracious acceptance of my coffee this morning I'm giving you the Bobby Fischer Charm Award."

THORNSBY is something you and your readers can't do without . . . and why should you, when you can have it so easily by collect phone, collect wire, or a postage due letter to . . .

THORNSBY

IS A CHARACTER YOUR READERS CAN IDENTIFY WITH.

He doesn't understand his hippy son . . . he's a bit confused by the lifestyles of the 70's . . . he's beset by taxes, pollution, and women's lib. His attempts to cope will make your readers on both sides of the generation gap laugh – at them– selves.

"He can't talk just now. He's busy recreating 1942."

"She stopped my Playboy subscription, but I've still got the movie ads."

"I knew I was overweight and I knew I had ulcers, but—'bad vibes!'"

"Well, it was rated PG!"

"He's the only one in town to learn from Reader's Digest that he may already be a loser."

"That's it. Hon   Hang in there!"

THORNSBY

A SURVIVAL KIT FOR THE 70's

2-column
6-a-week

"No doubt she's going brainless, too."

Here Comes

THORNSBY

"Let's put it this way, Hon—you'll never make Cosmopolitan."

"You see, Dad, instead of a Dean of Men or a Dean of Women, we have a Dean of Meaningful Relations."

"Say, I like that rhythm! It says: 'he's too fat, he's too fat, he's too fat' . . ."

NATIONAL NEWSPAPER SYNDICATE *Inc., of America* • 20 NORTH WACKER DRIVE, CHICAGO, ILLINOIS, 60606 • Telephone 312-782-1393 • ROBERT C. DILLE, President

NATIONAL NEWSPAPER SYNDICATE Inc., of America

20 NORTH WACKER DRIVE • CHICAGO 6
STate 2-1393 • ROBERT C. DILLE, President

N N S

All material © Nat'l. Newsp. Synd., Inc.

EDITORIAL POLICY

In the interests of flexibility NATIONAL grants permission to shorten copy when necessary. We ask only that the authors' personalities and meanings be preserved carefully.

If a substantial error appears on NATIONAL's copy, or if you have a question, feel free to call collect, STate 2-1393, Chicago.

Fred McLaren -- Creator of THORNSBY

Fred McLaren has been a nut about cartoons since he was ten years old. That was the year he started his cartoon collection--with a huge, ten-foot-long drawing of three elves named Snap, Crackle and Pop.

"I walked into my local grocery store," he recalls, "and saw this fantastic cartoon by Vernon Grant, a famous cartoonist and an idol of mine. I told the grocer I had to have it. He was so flabbergasted he couldn't refuse."

For many years the elves hung from wall to wall over McLaren's bed--until they disappeared after he left home to serve in the Army during the Korean War. But by that time he had long since made up his mind that collecting cartoons was not enough--he wanted to draw his own.

In 1954 he entered the American Academy of Art in Chicago. For three years he studied drawing and painting under William Mosby, a famous instructor and top illustrator. At the same time, he and a friend created "Captain Shark," a new adventure comic strip based under the seas. It never caught on.

After finishing art school, McLaren went into commercial art. He served as art director on various magazines, then began doing graphic design for advertising and promotion work in the mid-1960's. His cartoons were featured in Sylvania's national advertising campaigns in 1971 and 1972, and his free-lance humorous illustrations were published in books, house organs and Sunday supplements.

Meanwhile the idea for THORNSBY was slowly developing in the back of his mind. "I've been fascinated by the way people react when they find themselves becoming middle-aged," McLaren says. "They look around and they're amazed to find that they're in a world they never made. Thornsby is like that. He's an average guy who's faced with strange-looking kids, women's lib, pollution, and cars that are always breaking down. He didn't make it--it just happened."

McLaren denies that THORNSBY is an autobiographical sketch, but friends note a lot of similarities. Like his cartoon character, McLaren is a nostalgia nut. He collects old comics, pulp magazines, books and radio tapes; and his pride and joy is a 1955 Morgan sports car. With his wife and two sons, he lives in New Lenox, Illinois.

# # #

Fred's National Newspaper Syndicate biography distributed to the press and newspapers carrying Thornsby.

A series of promotional ad mats distributed to newspapers to publicize the launch of Thornsby in their local paper.

A CARTOON IS BORN

IT COULD BE YOU

Have you ever looked in the mirror and discovered that you're growing older? Have you looked around and noticed that things are not quite turning out as you expected?

That's what happened to cartoonist Fred McLaren, and he reacted by creating THORNSBY, a new daily cartoon panel.

Follow Thornsby and his family as they confront high taxes, traffic jams, pollution and all the other aggravations we all face.

THORNSBY

"They can't wait for **THORNSBY,** the new cartoon panel, to start on Monday."

LAUGH WITH THORNSBY DAILY IN

"It's not another protest, they just want to make sure
THORNSBY, the new cartoon panel, starts on Monday."

"It's not another protest, they just want to make sure
THORNSBY, the new cartoon panel, starts on Monday."

Don't miss Thornsby!
Starts Monday in The Daily News

Promotional ad published in the Chicago Daily News. March 1974.

Promotional ad published in the Lincoln, Nebraska newspaper.
January 14, 1974.

"... Signed up for ceramics and basket weaving and have a groovy roommate—38-26-37—so college seems well worth your money ..."

Thornsby

"I presume you want it fileted?"

Hazel

Hazel and Thornsby: two new faces on the Comics/Columns/Puzzles pages.

Hazel, everybody's favorite maid, and Thornsby, the middle-aged middle American who's continually befuddled by his fast-changing world, are two big additions to The Observer's new Comics/Columns/Puzzles pages beginning Monday, July 30.

Ellen Peck, "Seek and Find," and "Trivia Quiz" will also be a part of the whole new look. Look for the Comics/Columns/Puzzles pages coming July 30.

The Charlotte Observer

A New Look On The Comic Pages

DEAR READERS:

Today we offer The Observer's new-look Comics pages, designed for easier reading and presenting four exciting new features to join Bettle Bailey. Snuffy Smith, Jim Bishop, Erma Bombeck and your other old favorites.

Remember Hazel, the cantankerous maid who first became an American institution in the Saturday Evening Post? She's joining our lineup of cartoons, along with a delightfully befuddled fellow named Thornsby, who hasn't quite figured

out his hippy son, his liberated daughter or the 1970s in general.

Ellen Peck and Dr. E. James Lieberman team up three days a week to provide honest answers to the problems of teen-agers and their families. And there's an intriguing new word puzzle called "Seek & Find."

Look for these newcomers — plus our regular lineup of 20 comic strips. Dr. Van Dellen, the Aces on Bridge, Carroll Righter's Horoscope, Today's Crossword, Joyce Lain Kennedy's Career Corner and a Q-and-A quiz — this week. Today's Comics pages are on pages 6-7B. We think you'll like them a lot.

THE EDITORS

Promotional ads published in the Charlotte, North Carolina newspaper. July 23-30, 1973.

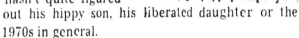
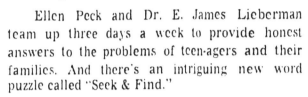
47

New for You

Thornsby in Journal

Cartoonist
McLaren

Fred McLaren is the creator of a new Journal cartoon. He's always been interested in drawing and the character of Thornsby slowly developed in his mind. "I've been fascinated by the way people react when they find themselves becoming middle-aged. They look around and they're amazed to find that they're in a world they never made. Thornsby is like that."

Today on Page 44

Promotional article in the Lincoln, Nebraska newspaper. January 9, 1974.

Thornsby: In Above His Head

New Cartoon Added To Star-Herald Line-Up

A new daily cartoon — THORNSBY — one of the funniest laugh panels to come on the newspaper scene in recent years, is making its debut in today's Star-Herald and will become a regular feature.

Today is the first time this new cartoon has been seen, and newspapers across the nation are including it among their entertainment packages.

Artist Homer Frederick McLaren is the very image of his subject. THORNSBY is today. He is relevant, he is "now," and he is here now in the Star-Herald.

THORNSBY is an anachronism, as out-of-time and out-of-place in today's world as he can be.

McLaren sees the funny side of those little, and not so little, confrontations and confusions that comprise the happenings of our every waking hour. THORNSBY is aimed at readers "over 30," but the younger generations also can see in him their fathers, uncles and grandfathers. Women can see in him their husbands.

In explaining the idea for THORNSBY, artist McLaren says: "I've been fascinated by the way people react when they find themselves become middle-aged. They look around and they're amazed to find that they're in a world they never made. Thornsby is like that. He's an average guy who's faced with strange-looking kids, women's lib, pollution, and cars that are always breakingn. He didn't make it — it just happened."

Inside Today

A 20-page special section of today's Star-Herald outlines some of the development projects currently underway or planned in the community, and some of the problems of the cities in coping with a growing population and economy.

Promotional story in the Scottsbluff, Nebraska newspaper. April 15, 1973.

Thornsby was published in a larger format on the Editorial page of the Boston Herald. Quite a coup for any cartoonist, usually reserved for political strips like "Doonesbury" by Garry Trudeau.

Regarding a recent "Thornsby" cartoon on The Daily News comic page — one depicting Thornsby sitting in his nostalgia-cluttered den, and captioned, "And you're always bugging me about keeping my room clean!"—the items in the den included a pennant reading "Austin High" and, on a stack of magazines, a football bearing the score "Austin 12, Tech 7." Now, when I was a senior at Austin, back in 1918, our class president was a Joseph McLaren, and I was wondering if the "Thornsby" cartoonist, Fred McLaren, comes from the Austin neighborhood McLaren family.—A.D., LaGrange

T h o r n s b y ' s den: Why "Austin High"?

No, Fred McLaren, who now lives in Canada, comes from a Springfield (Ill.) McLaren family. Nevertheless—the pennant and football in Thornsby's den indirectly do relate to Chicago's Austin High. McLaren is a jazz aficionado, and a popular jazz group of the late '20s was "The Chicagoans," which started as the "Austin High Gang," students at the school. Members of the Austin High Gang and, later, the Chicagoans, included such well-known musicians as Frank Teschemacher, Jimmy McPartland and Bud Freeman. When McLaren was penciling out the cartoon, the name "Austin High" just "seemed to fit," he said. Presumably, nostalgia freak Thornsby, like his creator, is also a jazz aficionado.

Reader question & answer in the Chicago Daily News, tracing the Chicago roots of Thornsby's frequent references to Austin High. 1974.

Dentist's Mail Missing

Sir: It is beyond my comprehension how you can disallow the education of the public to good, preventive dentistry by eliminating the excellent articles which have previously filled your papers in the Dentist's Mailbox.

The general public is illiterate when it comes to good, preventive dentistry and my office staff and I were totally excited to see your articles each Monday morning that were helping people to understand themselves better. Suddenly, that little bit of realization that you gave them is gone.

Not that this void in dental education wasn't enough, I found a cute little cartoon (Thornsby) in the July 9 paper. Let me describe it for you. A sign on the wall "Jimmy Soregums Dental Surgeon" and a bandaged-mouthed patient crawling out of the dental office with the dental nurse pulling him by the back of of his neck. And you want people to take care of themselves by visiting their dentist regularly?

Aren't there enough people in this world with missing teeth that should never have had such a thing happen? Your paper could help. Why doesn't it?

Stanley L. Becker, D.D.S.
Baltimore.

Letter to the Editor in The Baltimore Sun complaining about the portrayal of dentists in the media, and referencing that "cute little cartoon" Thornsby. August 2, 1973.

Oh Happy Day! Comics Return

LOST or STRAYED: One large Great Dane; answers to the name of MARMADUKE; last seen in the vicinity of 7505 Warwick Blvd.; sadly missed by elderly woman; if found, return to Daily Press. No questions asked.

FOUND: One large, spindly-legged dog; refuses to answer any questions until he sees his lawyer. ALSO FOUND: a number of peculiar children, including one particularly vicious straw-haired boy (a menace to the community); one puckish, balding, middle-aged man; other undesirable types. TO CLAIM: Pick up a Daily Press anytime after Monday, April 8.

If you are like Dorothy Crane of Hampton, who sent in the LOST ad above, you will be glad to hear that "Marmaduke," "Family Circle," "Dennis the Menace," "Better Half," and "Thornsby" will return to the pages of the Daily Press this Monday. They were temporarily discontinued because of the paper shortage. Sorry.

Announcement in the Newport News, Virginia newspaper referencing the return of Thornsby following a temporary paper shortage.

April 4, 1974.

Letter to the Editor in the Detroit Free Press bemoaning the demise of Thornsby.

December 26, 1975.

As Our Readers See It

No Joke

TO REPLACE the delightful "Thornsby" with an exercise of daily alcoholic excess, "Fogarty," was a grave editorial mistake. Alcoholism is not funny. It is a dreadful disease and should not be a source of misdirected humor. I am disappointed in your judgment.

TIMOTHY S. WATSON
Grand Rapids

PUBLICITY

Drawing cartoons replaces earlier collecting hobby

Fred McLaren

Fred McLaren was a ten-year-old kid when he started a cartoon collection with a ten-foot drawing of three elves—Snap, Crackle and Pop—wangled from the local grocery store. The treasure hung wall to wall above his bed until he left home for Army service in the Korean War.

By the time McLaren got out of the Army he had long since decided he wanted to draw cartoons instead of collect them and went off to the American Academy of Art in Chicago. As a student he and a friend created an adventure comic strip which never caught on.

McLaren's field after graduation was commercial art and in the mid 60s he began doing graphic design for advertising and promotion work while his freelance humorous illustrations were published in books, house organs and Sunday supplements.

Meantime, the idea for a newspaper panel slowly developed. Tom Hirsh, his editor at National Newspaper Syndicate in Chicago, thinks the newly launched McLaren panel hero, "Thornsby," is really the cartoonist himself. But McLaren thinks not so.

Still, Hirsh points out that McLaren is a nostalgia nut who collects old comics, pulp magazines, books and radio tapes and is fascinated by sports cars. So is "Thornsby." McLaren's pride and joy is a 1955 Morgan sports car. The cartoonist and his wife and two sons live in New Lenox, Illinois.

"Thornsby" grew into a daily cartoon panel out of Fred McLaren's confessed fascination with the way people react when they find themselves middle-aged. "They look around and they're amazed to find that they're in a world they never made. Thornsby is like that. He's an average guy who's faced with strange-looking kids, women's lib, pollution and cars that are always breaking down."

AMA honors science ed

Two newspaper series on mental health problems and heart transplants have won for David Hendin, editor of Enterprise Science News, a 1972 Medical Journalism Award from the American Medical Association. Hendin will receive the $1000 prize next month during the AMA convention in New York City. The science editor is the author of four books including the current best-seller, "Death as a Fact of Life."

4- and 5-col. daily strip. Four sizes of 4-col

"Remember when we danced to the same music?"

EDITOR & PUBLISHER for May 19, 1973

Story in the "Editor & Publisher" trade magazine. May 19, 1973.

≈ THE ROUGH RIDER

THORNSBY by Fred McLaren is a featurer of the National Newspaper Syndicate. The creator of the cartoon is Fred McLaren, London, Ontario, Canada. Fred is the owner of a '55 twin spare roadster (which is somehow reflected in the adventures of Thornsby) and a member of MCC.

For you COMIX freaks, Fred was the creator of "Captain Shark" in the mid '50s. Since then, some general commercial art activities, illustration and art direction of various magazines. The idea of Thornsby , "I've been fascinated by the way people react when they find themselves becoming middle-aged," McLaren says. "They look around and they're amazed to find that they're in a world they never made. Thornsby is like that. He's an average guy who's faced with strange-looking kids, women's lib, pollution, and cars that are always breaking down. He didn't make it--it just happened."

If you see a fellow who looks like the chap in cartoon 1, ("You just had to ask) driving a Black '55 roadster, that's Fred

EZ

Fred and Thornsby's love for their prized Morgan sports car was honored by the Morgan Car Club fanzine titled "The Rough Rider."

" YOU HAD TO ASK!"

"It's as if our garage gets pregnant every summer!"

"Sure it's a toy, but he says it makes up for that electric train he never got!"

"O.K. THESE LITTLE ENGLISH JOBS CAN TAKE ANY HILL, BUT CAN YOU GET IT DOWN?"

THE ROUGH RIDER 2
1975

"Let's put it this way. Hon. you'll never make Cosmopolitan."

"Well, it finally happened. They invaded even both year on the same day."

"Try to understand, Dear. He'll never go for Harry James."

"Say, I like that rhythm! It says: 'he's too fat, he's too fat, he's too fat'..."

New Lenox cartoonist
tickles nation's funnybone

By DAVE BOGDAN
Herald-News Writer

NEW LENOX — Buck Rogers, Dick Tracy, Peanuts and Dennis the Menace are cartoon characters that have become famous. Mr. Thornsby may be added to the list of famous cartoon characters one day.

Thornsby is the creation of Fred McLaren, 43, of 1304 Oak St. in New Lenox. It is a syndicated cartoon panel published six days a week by newspapers throughout the United States.

"I hope that Thornsby will someday become as much of a household word as many of the other cartoon characters have become," said McLaren. "There is no hidden message involved with Thornsby. I leave the hidden messages to the political cartoonists. Thornsby is just intended to be entertaining.

"There has never really been a cartoon panel just like Thornsby before," said McLaren. "He is a character that a middle aged person in the middle class can identify with. He is caught in a world of changing conditions."

Some cartoon characters are an indirect or direct reflection of the artist himself or his family and friends.

"Thornsby is characterized to be older than I am," said McLaren. "But I have to admit that Thornsby's problems and reactions are often my own, but Thornsby isn't exactly an autobiographical character.

"Thornsby is a man living in the 1970's, but he doesn't know how he got there. He is still thinking in the 1940's. Thornsby isn't a loser though and he is determined to hand in there. He has weaknesses that many people can identify with."

McLaren said that the other characters in the Thornsby cartoon panel are composite characters.

"Thornsby's children were developed by combining all the children I know. My own children and their friends were a great influence. Thornsby's wife isn't a direct reflection of my wife. But my wife is similar to Mrs. Thornsby in some ways.

"There are other characters in the Thornsby cartoon that appear quite often because I think it is necessary to have more than the family situation. You need to have other characters with definite personality traits or the cartoons will become boring after a while."

Thornsby is distributed by the National Newspaper Syndicate Inc. of America, a Chicago firm, and was first run April 16, 1972 in the St. Louis Post Dispatch. It is now published in several other large newspapers, such as the Detroit Free Press, Philadelphia Bulletin and Boston Herald American, as well as many smaller newspapers.

"Having Thornsby get started in the St. Louis Post Dispatch was great," said McLaren. "It was a big break in my life to have the cartoon published. And getting Thornsby in several other large papers helped some of the smaller papers pick it up. The cartoon is running well in the eastern states and is beginning to spread across the country."

McLaren was born and raised in Springfield, but moved to Chicago following service in the United States Army during the Korean War.

He studied at the American Academy in Chicago from 1954 to 1957 under Bill Mosly.

"Mosly is a well known instructor," said McLaren. "He helped me a great deal, especially with the fundamentals of drawing. I studied illustrating and fine arts at the American Academy."

McLaren attempted to get a cartoon syndicated as soon as he completed study at the American Academy.

"In 1957 I was working on a continuous type comic strip called Captain Shark," said McLaren. "Captain Shark was a typical square, lantern-jawed face guy and the strip was about oceanology. I tried to get the strip syndicated, but nobody wanted it. The continuing story comic strips aren't as popular as they used to be.

"Then, in 1959, I came up with another idea for a cartoon. It was based on beatniks. The cartoon was a single panel, gag-a-day cartoon like Thornsby.

But I feel on my nose again. The idea was received much better than Captain Shark and the people I talked to seemed to like it. I was encouraged by their response," said McLaren.

McLaren went into the commercial art business for 10 years after his second failure to get into the syndicated cartoon business. He worked in advertising and publications for several different companies.

"Even when I was in the commercial art business, I did cartooning on the side," said McLaren. "I kept working on cartoons all the time and it was in the back of my mind all the time to attempt getting a cartoon syndicated."

McLaren moved to New Lenox in 1961.

"I liked doing cartooning so well. I never gave up," said McLaren. "My drawing was getting better all the time and I had enough faith in myself and determination, that I kept trying. You have to pay the price of working hard to get what you want sometimes."

McLaren first thought of Thornsby a couple of years ago.

"The kind of cartoon Thornsby is I couldn't have done when I first got out of college," said McLaren. "It reflects things that I see happening now, looking from the age I am now. I can see the generation gap, pollution and all the other problems now that I didn't see quite the same before.

"I think it helped me to get banged around for a while by the syndicates. I am much older and wiser now than when I first got out of college. Thornsby evolved and I evolved. Thornsby fell together nicely, but there is no way to do it all overnight. Cartooning isn't like casting a Hollywood movie," said McLaren.

McLaren said it is hard to get into the syndicated cartoon business because of competition with the standard cartoons.

"Right from the beginning you are competing against the standards," said McLaren. "There is only so much room in the papers for comics. So many of the artists that have been in the cartoon business from the beginning are still around. Dick Tracy, Blondie and Flash Gordon have become institutions in the business. You have to come up with a good idea that is different from the standards.

"A cartoonist has to be pretty darn good to make it in the syndicated cartoon business," said McLaren.

McLaren claims that his two biggest influences were Vernon Grant and Jack Davis.

"I don't draw like either one of them, but they both had a big influence on me," said McLaren. "Grant was a famous advertising cartoonist when I was growing up. He did the Snap, Crackle and Pop cartoon for Rice Crispies. He also did many magazine covers. I collected a great amount of his work.

"Davis does work for many magazines, such as Mad and Time. When I was in art school he was drawing horror comics, which brought on a comics code. The code bans material from comics that is thought to be a bad influence on children," said McLaren.

McLaren thinks cartoons are the best business for a cartoonist.

"Cartooning is a totally creative thing, unlike most things a creative artist does," said McLaren. "You start out with a white sheet of paper and nobody can help you.

"The drawing is just fun. The work part is the writing of the captions. I think of myself as a cartoonist and writer. I know how my characters talk," said McLaren.

McLaren thinks the writing of the captions is much more difficult and important than the drawing.

"There are many people that can draw equally as well as the other people in the cartoon business," said McLaren. "But the writing comes first. The cartoon has to be funny.

"I write all of the time. Sometimes the ideas come in bundles. Then I make a sketch of who will be in the panel. I try to do one cartoon each day and keep eight weeks ahead of schedule all the time," said McLaren.

"You see, Dad, instead of a Dean of Men or a Dean of Women, we have a Dean of Meaningful Relations."

"Why, it's Mr. Thornsby!"

"She stopped my Playboy subscription, but I've still got the movie ads."

"I knew I was overweight and I knew I had skers, but bad vibes?"

Fred McLaren cartoons printed
with permission of
National Newspaper Syndicate Inc. of America

New Lenox cartoonist

tickles nation's funnybone

By DAVE BOGDAN
Herald News Writer

NEW LENOX – Buck Rogers, Dick Tracy, Peanuts and Dennis the Menace are cartoon characters that have become famous. Mr. Thornsby may be added to the list of famous cartoon characters one day.

Thornsby is the creation of Fred McLaren, 43, of 134 Oak St. in New Lenox. It is a syndicated cartoon panel published six days a week by newspapers throughout the United States.

"I hope that Thornsby will someday become as much of a household word as many of the other cartoon characters have become," said McLaren. "There is no hidden message involved with Thornsby. I leave the hidden messages to the political cartoonists. Thornsby is just intended to be entertaining."

"There has never really been a cartoon panel just like Thornsby before," said McLaren. "He is a character that a middle aged person in the middle class can identify with. He is caught in a world of changing conditions."

Some cartoon characters are an indirect or direct reflection of the artist himself or his family and friends.

"Thornsby is characterized to be older than I am," said McLaren. "But I have to admit that Thornsby's problems and reactions are often my own, but Thornsby isn't exactly an autobiographical character."

"Thornsby is a man living in the 1970s, but he doesn't know how he got there. He is still thinking in the 1940s. Thornsby isn't a loser though and he is determined to hang in there. He has weaknesses that many people can identify with."

McLaren said that the other characters in the Thornsby cartoon panel are composite characters.

"Thornsby's wife isn't a direct reflection of my wife. But my wife is similar to Mrs. Thornsby in some ways."

"There are other characters in the Thornsby cartoon that appear quite often because I think it is necessary to have more than the family situation. You need to have other characters with definite personality traits or the cartoons will become boring after a while."

Thornsby is distributed by the National Newspaper Syndicate Inc. of America, a Chicago firm, and was first run April 16, 1973 in the St. Louis Post-Dispatch. It is now published in several other large newspapers, such as the Detroit Free Press, Philadelphia Bulletin and Boston Herald American, as well as many smaller newspapers.

"Having Thornsby get started in the St. Louis Post-Dispatch was great," said McLaren. "It was a big break in my life to have the cartoon published. And getting Thornsby in several other large papers helped some of the smaller papers pick it up. The cartoon is running well in the eastern states and is beginning to spread across the country."

McLaren was born and raised in Springfield, but moved to Chicago following service in the United States Army during the Korean War.

He studied at the American Academy in Chicago from 1954 to 1957 under Bill Mosby.

"Mosby is a well know instructor," said McLaren. "He helped me a great deal, especially with the fundamentals of drawing. I studied illustrating and fine arts at the American Academy."

McLaren attempted to get a cartoon syndicated as soon as he completed study at the American Academy. *[Continued on next page]*

[Continued from previous page]   "In 1957, I was working on a continuous-type comic called Captain Shark," said McLaren. "Captain Shark was a typical square lantern-jawed face guy and the strip was about oceanology. I tried to get the strip syndicated, but nobody wanted it. The continuing story comic strips aren't as popular as they used to be."

"Then, in 1959, I came up with another idea for a cartoon. It was based on beatniks. The cartoon was a single-panel, gag-a-day cartoon like Thornsby. But I fell on my nose again. The idea was received much better than Captain Shark and the people I talked to seemed to like it. I was encouraged by their response," said McLaren.

McLaren went into the commercial art business for 10 years after his second failure to get into the syndicated cartoon business. He worked in advertising and publications for several different companies.

"Even when I was in the commercial art business, I did cartooning on the side," said McLaren. "I kept working on cartoons all the time and it was in the back of my mind all the time to attempt getting a cartoon syndicated."

McLaren moved to New Lenox in 1961.

"I liked doing cartooning so well, I never gave up," said McLaren. "My drawing was getting better all the time and I had enough faith in myself and determination, that I kept trying. You have to pay the price of working hard to get what you want sometimes."

McLaren first thought of Thornsby a couple of years ago. "The kind of cartoon Thornsby is I couldn't have done when I first got out of college." said McLaren. "It reflects things that I see happening now, looking from the age I am now. I can see the generation gap, pollution and all the other problems now that I didn't see quite the same before."

"I think it helped me to get banged around for a while by the syndicates. I am much older and wiser now than when I first got out of college. Thornsby evolved and I evolved. Thornsby fell together nicely. But there is no way to do it all overnight. Cartooning isn't like casting a Hollywood movie," said McLaren.

McLaren said it is hard to get into the syndicated cartoon business because of competition with the standard cartoons. "Right from the beginning you are competing against the standard," said McLaren. "There is only so much room in the papers for comics. So many of the artists that have been in the cartoon business from the beginning are still around. Dick Tracy, Blondie and Flash Gordon have become institutions in the business. You have to come up with a good idea that is different from the standards."

"A cartoonist has to be pretty damn good to make it in the syndicated cartoon business," said McLaren.

McLaren claims that his two biggest influences were Vernon Grant and Jack Davis.

"I can't draw like either one of them, but they both had a big influence on me," said McLaren. "Grant was a famous advertising cartoonist when I was growing up. He did the Snap, Crackle and Pop cartoon for Rice Krispies. He also did many magazine covers. I collected a great amount of his work."

"Davis does work for many magazines, such as "Mad" and "Time." When I was in art school he was drawing horror comics, which brought on a comics code. The code bans material from comics that is thought to be a bad influence on children," said McLaren.

McLaren thinks cartoons are the best business for a cartoonist.

"Cartooning is a totally creative thing, unlike most things a creative artist does," said McLaren. "You start out with a white sheet of paper and nobody can help you."

"The drawing is just fun. The work part is the writing of the captions. I think of myself as a cartoonist and writer. I know how my characters talk," said McLaren.

McLaren thinks the writing of the captions is much more difficult and important than the drawing.

"There are many people that can draw equally as well as the other people in the cartoon business," said McLaren. "But the writing comes first. The cartoon has to be funny."

"I write all of the time. Sometimes the ideas come in bundles. Then I make a sketch of who will be in the panel. I try to do one cartoon each day and keep eight weeks ahead of schedule all the time," said McLaren.

SKETCHES

Rough sketches were often penciled prior to work on the final cartoon. Only a few of these sketches were kept for posterity.

First draft of the comic published December 29, 1973.

First draft of the comic published April 19, 1974.

First draft of the comic published May 8, 1974.

First draft of the comic published August 2, 1973.

Fred used his profile caricature throughout his entire life, both professionally (as a logo on his freelance business cards and letterhead) and personally (in lieu of his signature on letters and cards). Look for it in the foreground and background of many Thornsby cartoons.

"At your age, with your eyes getting weak, and your teeth falling out and your heart running down, all I can tell you is: pay cash on your way out."

The first published cartoon. April 16, 1973.

Chapter 2

Thornsby: Published Newspaper Run

Assembled here for the first time, the complete newspaper run of Thornsby consists of 768 cartoons, published between April 16, 1973 and September 27, 1975. It ran 6 days per week, Monday through Saturday. Each comic has been scanned from the best available source: original art drawings, proof sheet mats, and newspaper clippings.

Fred's personal collection, at the time of his death, consisted of 375 original cartoons. His handwritten captions are often visible beneath the typeset caption glued to the original artwork. The originals absent from his private collection were disbursed through the years to family, friends, and fans of Thornsby. High quality proof sheets were also (fortunately) stored in his collection and covered the majority of the run. Newspaper clippings were needed to fill in a few missing dates.

Various newspapers would occasionally substitute a different (previously published) cartoon on any given day, for reasons often unknown. Thornsby did tackle controversial subjects and feature provocative female drawings that were often more suitable to an adult audience. Some conservative newspaper editors chose to replace cartoons that referenced pot smoking and featured braless women. The subjects and images seem tame by today's standards, but this was the 1970s, a decade when open-mindedness was just starting to emerge.

Look closely at the detail in the drawings. Much of the humor lies in the background visuals, whether it's a headline in the newspaper Thornsby is holding or a poster hanging on the wall behind the characters. Many readers assume the caption always tells the whole story, which is true for the majority of newspaper comics. Thornsby however, provided additional laughs in the drawings themselves, which were filled with inside jokes, sight gags, and other topical references to the world at that time. When reproduced as a small image on a newspaper's comic page, most people missed the humor in these details. This book gives everyone a fresh look at Fred's brilliant artwork and razor-sharp wit.

To those viewing Thornsby for the first time: the comic was not always politically correct by today's standards, but it is a part of history and a function of its time. Thornsby was a middle aged man living in the Midwest in the mid 1970s. For those of us who are old enough to remember, it was a different era, indeed!

"At your age, with your eyes getting weak, and your teeth falling out and your heart running down, all I can tell you is: pay cash on your way out."

April 16, 1973

A few newspapers published this comic in advance on Sunday, April 15th, to promote the official launch of Thornsby on Monday, April 16th.

Fred never understood the appeal of jogging and so, he never participated in this trend.

April 17, 1973

"Never make the team."

"Why, it's Mr. Thornsby!"

April 18, 1973

Thornsby loved his girlie magazines - one of the comic's most frequently used themes. Look for "Playboy," "Penthouse," "Oui," and a slew of other magazines with witty made-up titles in the artwork of many future cartoons.

April 19, 1973

"When dual buzzers ring, fasten seatbelts, lower back windows, turn key 45 degrees to the north and take two aspirin."

"... and so I appeal to the silent majority. During the next four years you will remain silent."

April 20, 1973

Never one to shy away from politics, Thornsby occasionally featured President Nixon (see the caricature on the TV screen) and many other real-life politicians.

Thornsby's prized Morgan sports car appeared so frequently that it became one of the comic's central characters. It is a tribute to Fred's own 1955 Morgan sports car.

April 21, 1973

"Oh no! Not another childhood!"

"He's the only one in town to learn from Reader's Digest that he may already be a loser."

April 23, 1973

Fred numbered the first 24 Thornsby cartoons (in this example, see the #13 in the lower right corner), but the syndicator did not run them in this sequential order.

The first of numerous appearances of Jimmy Soregums, DDS, and his sadistic assistant Rancid.   The dentist and the medical doctor (who started with the May 1, 1973 comic) were Thornsby's most widely used recurring characters.

April 24, 1973

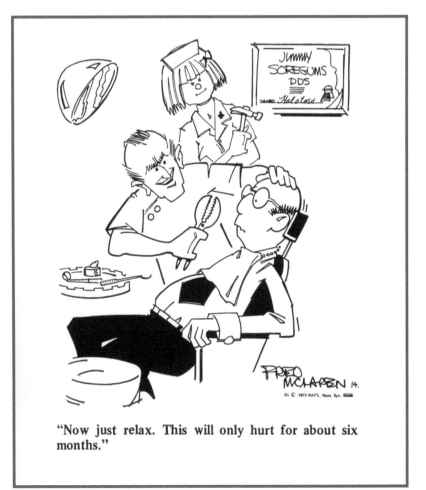

"Now just relax. This will only hurt for about six months."

"Remember when we danced to the same music?"

April 25, 1973

One of Fred's favorite Thornsby comics. He framed the St. Louis Post-Dispatch newspaper clipping and displayed it through his retired years. St. Louis had the only newspaper which colorized its weekday comics.

Fred tested the limits of what conservative American newspapers would publish with his semi-nude young women, often in barely-there bikinis or very tight braless tops.

April 26, 1973

"You've had enough dear. Let's go home before you have a cardiac arrest."

70

"I can't cope either. But *I'm* enjoying it!"

April 27, 1973

The first of several comics with a (then controversial) marijuana theme. During the 1960s and 1970s, pot usage was more common with the younger generation than their parent's generation.

April 28, 1973

"Here, try something different: tobacco!"

April 30, 1973

"No."

The first appearance of popular recurring characters Amorphous Dread, MD, and his sexy nurse.

May 1, 1973

"I don't know what you've got, but here's a prescription you can't read for medicine that may or may not work."

May 2, 1973

"Of course not, silly. He's just overweight."

May 3, 1973

"There must be *one* I wouldn't be too embarrassed to pay for."

"Oh, I don't know. She looks about 18 to me."

May 4, 1973

The first of many comics that include Fred as himself (in this instance, as a friend of Thornsby). Note he's carrying his art portfolio (art imitates life).

May 5, 1973

"Perhaps it's just that they identify with you."

"Say, I like that rhythm! It says: 'he's too fat, he's too fat, he's too fat' . . ."

May 7, 1973

According to the United States Flag Code, the American flag should never be used as wearing apparel.

May 8, 1973

"That's okay, fella, you don't have to salute."

"... The chance of measurable precipitation is 80%, the chance of a thundershower is 10%, your chance, in case of nuclear attack, is 1.5% ..."

May 9, 1973

This cartoon was a precursor to US National Security Advisor Henry Kissinger ordering a DEF-CON-3 alert on October 24, 1973, in response to reports that the USSR was preparing to defend Egypt in its war with Israel.

"Love Story" is the tear-jerking 1970 feature film that became one of the highest-grossing movies of all time.

May 10, 1973

"She's all set for another showing of 'Love Story'!"

May 11, 1973

"It was a good day—no protests, no riots, no pollution, and our new car made it home without falling apart."

May 12, 1973

"Have a real nice Monday morning, Dear."

"Let's put it this way, Hon—you'll never make Cosmopolitan."

May 14, 1973

"Cosmopolitan" magazine gained publicity and popularity in the 1970s by featuring Burt Reynolds in a nude centerfold.

Car recalls became a common occurrence starting in the 1970s, impacting the daily lives of millions of automobile owners.

This cartoon also features the first of several appearances of Fred's profile caricature in the background crowd.

May 15, 1973

"Well, it finally happened . . . They recalled everybody's car on the same day."

May 16, 1973

"I knew I was overweight and I knew I had ulcers, but—
'bad vibes'?"

May 17, 1973

"That's it, Hon. Hang in there!"

"She stopped my Playboy subscription, but I've still got the movie ads."

May 18, 1973

The first of numerous appearances of Thornsby's neighbor Grim Jim. His name never appeared in the captions, but it can be traced back to the comic's original pitch deck.

Thornsby has a stack of Big Little Books next to him. These small compact books were first published in 1932 with "The Adventures of Dick Tracy." Fred actively collected Big Little Books throughout his life.

May 19, 1973

"He can't talk just now. He's busy recreating 1942."

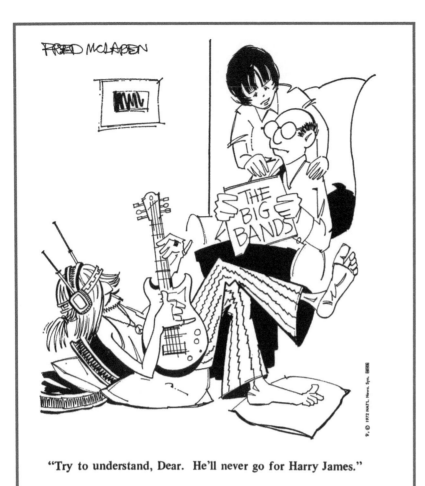

"Try to understand, Dear. He'll never go for Harry James."

May 21, 1973

Next to Frank Sinatra, Fred's favorite musician was Harry James - the legendary trumpet-playing bandleader who formed his big band in 1939. Fred's love of jazz and big band music was another commonly used theme throughout the Thornsby run.

May 22, 1973

". . . Signed up for ceramics and basket weaving and have a groovy roommate—38-26-37—so college seems well worth your money . . .

"Well, it *was* rated PG!"

May 23, 1973

1970s movies aimed at adults were notorious for including violence and nudity. Note the inclusion of the Dirty Old Man character next to Thornsby.

Long hair for men was all the rage at this time in the 1970s. Self-portrait of Fred in the lower right corner.

May 24, 1973

"For your gracious acceptance of my coffee this morning I'm giving you the Bobby Fischer Charm Award."

May 25, 1973

The World Chess Championship of 1972 made controversial chess champion Bobby Fischer and his opponent Boris Spassky into household names.

May 26, 1973

"You see, Dad, instead of a Dean of Men or a Dean of Women, we have a Dean of Meaningful Relations."

"Come on out, Thornsby. We promise not to call you 'sickie' anymore."

May 28, 1973

'Sickie' was a word that Fred frequently used and loved. He recycled it again in the July 13, 1973 caption.

The resurgence of Universal Monster movie reruns on late night television was enjoyed by the McLaren family during the early 1970s (particularly by Fred's son Tom).

May 29, 1973

" . . . And now for the conclusion of 'Son of Frankenstein.'"

May 30, 1973

"Your inheritance was worth $500,000. But after back taxes, state and federal taxes, and my fee, you'll still clear a dollar ninety-eight."

In the early 1970s, airline hijackings were a frighteningly common phenomenon. Airport security would increase in subsequent decades, but the 9/11 disaster would prove how weak the system still was at that point in time.

May 31, 1973

"Coffee, tea or tranquilizers?"

June 1, 1973

"Why do they worry about cleansing their minds? They haven't cleansed their clothes since 1970?"

A full-size proof sheet of this cartoon shows Fred's original handwritten caption.

June 2, 1973

"NOW DON'T GET UPSET, DEAR. MAYBE HE'S GOT A GOOD JOB"

June 4, 1973

"Now what is that supposed to mean? You have to go to the bathroom?"

June 5, 1973

"Either you throw that thing out or I'm going to buy every girlie magazine in town!"

June 6, 1973

"Ms." magazine (co-founded by Gloria Steinem) launched in 1972 and became a symbol of the feminist movement. The first issue (as shown in this comic) had a 'Wonder Woman for President' cover story.

"Collier's" was a popular magazine during the first half of the twentieth century. After reaching its circulation peak in the 1940s, the publication ended in 1957.

June 7, 1973

"Of course I understand how it is with you. I used to sell Collier's."

"Now don't give me all that static about the technical superiority of Swedish movies!"

June 8, 1973

"I Am Curious (Yellow)" is one of many Swedish films seized by US Customs and banned in many states for a period of time.

June 9, 1973

"No doubt she's going brainless, too."

June 11, 1973

June 12, 1973

June 13, 1973

"This stuff is brand new and may have grim side effects, but for $50.00 I'll let you try it out."

June 14, 1973

"I thought you outgrew that trick thirty-five years ago!"

"Unisex is a plot to confuse bartenders. Pass it on."

June 15, 1973

Thornsby was very topical, with newspaper headlines always reflecting current events - in this instance, the Detroit auto industry's car recalls, as well as controversial public figures such as activist/actress Jane Fonda.

June 16, 1973

" . . . and so they decided to get together and talk over their problems."

"He's so proud of himself: six weeks without a cigarette!"

June 18, 1973

Fred was a lifelong smoker, starting in his teens and continuing for over 70 years.

June 19, 1973

"Got a light, weirdo?"

"Here comes Dr. Dread, but don't look his way. He charges $10 to say 'Good Morning.' "

June 20, 1973

Fred avoided medical doctors, only doing a handful of visits during his lifetime.

Ralph Nader emerged in the 1960s as a consumer advocate and became a well-known public figure in the 1970s.

June 21, 1973

"Don't mind him. Today's his day to play Ralph Nader."

"He thought 'The Grand Funk Railroad' was the sound of old steam trains."

June 22, 1973

Grand Funk Railroad rose to fame in the early 1970s with two number-one hit singles "We're an American Band" and "The Loco-motion."

Fred stuck to his conservative style of dress throughout his entire life.

June 23, 1973

"I think we'd both feel better if we knew there was a costume party going on."

June 25, 1973

"Yes, my son, there are many things we simply don't understand. Like why your recent contributions have been so small . . . "

Thornsby's humorless boss Gordon Darwin makes his first of several appearances.

Fred despised attending meetings during his corporate work years.

June 26, 1973

"Mr. Thornsby! While some of us may be delighted to remember who played Lamont Cranston on radio's 'The Shadow', this is *not* a trivia convention!"

"Sorry, Buddy, but it's the best I can do — I'm a skyjack dropout."

June 27, 1973

Fred didn't play golf. His favorite form of exercise was walking, which he did frequently up through his senior years.

June 28, 1973

"I think your trouble is 'follow through.'"

"Try not to get involved, Dear."

June 29, 1973

The rebellious 1960s began a cycle of protests that have continued to this very day. Many of the issues are still the same, decades later (look closely at the words on the protesters' signs).

Fred never participated in hunting as a form of recreational activity.

June 30, 1973

"Well, you did very well, Dear. With your $5,000 camper and your $200 rifle you got one little duck loaded with buckshot. You just made Hero of the Week!"

"Front four slightly sensitive."

Decrepit fortune teller Wilma Ouija was one of Fred's favorite characters. She was occasionally featured in his sketches given to family and friends during his retired years.

July 3, 1973

"I see you having as much trouble understanding this month as last. But wait! Next month will be worse!"

"Wonderful! Now's your chance to find out if they're really prejudiced against sports cars!"

July 4, 1973

Mark Spitz is an Olympic champion swimmer whose best-selling poster gained him sex symbol status after the 1972 Summer Olympics.

July 5, 1973

"Look out kids, here comes Mark Spitz!"

"GOTCHA!"

July 6, 1973

Fred served in the Korean War as an Army dental assistant at a base in Hawaii.

July 7, 1973

"I thought it was a nice, constructive hobby until I found out they were PLAYBOY playmates!"

"Next!"

July 9, 1973

Telephone companies came under fire in the 1970s due to various antitrust and operational issues. Lily Tomlin's most famous character is Ernestine, the brash telephone operator from TV's "Laugh-In" who lampooned 'Ma Bell.'

July 10, 1973

" . . . your call cannot go through as dialed. We are having another one of our hopelessly incompetent days."

"But I **can't** work. The mail is late, the phone is out of order and my typewriter has been recalled!"

July 11, 1973

The Miller Test is the US Supreme Court's test for determining whether speech or expression is obscenity appealing to the prurient interest.

July 12, 1973

"Psst! Prurient photos without redeeming social value?"

July 13, 1973

"Lovely after-dinner music—'The Sickie Sounds' Of The Acid-Rockers'!"

'Don't bring the kids to see Mona!' is the headline. Newspapers in this era ran titillating movie ads that were likely more entertaining than the movies themselves.

July 14, 1973

"Great choice of movies tonight—'Violence For Fun And Profit' or 'Hot Mona And Her Football Team!'"

" . . . and now fans, the lovely Lady Thornsby, here to accept her award as 'Sexbomb of the Year'!"

July 16, 1973

July 17, 1973

"Oh wow! What a little pay raise will do!"

"Leave the sideburns . . . I know they make me look like Joe Namath!"

July 18, 1973

Joe Namath, best known for his football career with the New York Jets, achieved celebrity status during the 1970s.

The St. Louis Post-Dispatch ran their comics in a rectangular, rather than square, orientation and cropped every Thornsby they published (for example, removing Fred's image on the left side of this particular comic).

July 19, 1973

" . . . Here's the clincher: 'Good until the first breakdown, recall, or 24 hours, whichever occurs first.'"

"There's a lot of that going around."

July 20, 1973

The psychiatrist Freudian Slips was only featured twice during Thornsby's run. A different psychiatrist named Instant Shrink was identified in the original pitch deck, but never used.

July 21, 1973

"I know this sounds silly, but last night I dreamed of becoming out of step with all those around me!"

July 23, 1973

"These days **nothing** works out right!"

Guy Lombardo was a bandleader well known for his New Year's Eve radio and TV specials.

Note the 'It's Tommy Tucker Time' album in the lower left. Tucker was a famous bandleader. Tommy Tucker was a nickname for son Tom in his early years.

July 24, 1973

"Gee, Dad, your Guy Lombardo records make me want to rush right out for a shave and a crewcut!"

"If I could only get it bugged once a month, think of the status!"

July 25, 1973

The Watergate scandal had everyone wondering if their own phone was being bugged. Hollywood popularized this trend with a series of 1970s paranoid thriller films like "All the President's Men."

July 26, 1973

"Blanche! A hair! I think I'm on the road back!"

"HANDY ANDY STRIKES AGAIN!"

July 27, 1973

'Handy Andy' was another phrase which Fred frequently used and enjoyed.

July 28, 1973

"O.K., let's play Twenty Questions. It's not an Indian, not a sailor, not a girl. What is it?"

July 30, 1973

"You know the diet's a success when you can read the dial all by yourself!"

July 31, 1973

"Two and a half hours behind a diesel—this must be my reward for giving up cigarettes!"

"Time for bifocals, Dear?"

August 1, 1973

Fred owned and treasured his collection of reel to reel tapes of old "Inner Sanctum" radio shows. And yes, he insisted the lights be turned off during playback.

August 2, 1973

"We're not allowed to use lights or watch TV when he plays tapes of old 'Inner Sanctum' shows."

"Now then, before we consider you for a promotion, the company will need a new Thornsby . . ."

August 3, 1973

August 4, 1973

"I'm trying to be patient—sooner or later the energy crisis will strike here!"

"Oh, his paunch connected to his kid-neys,
His kidneys connected to his ul-cers,
His ulcers connected to his leak-y heart . . . ."

August 6, 1973

Dr. Dread is holding sheet music touting: To the tune of 'Them Bones.' This is a reference to "Dem Bones," a popular and catchy spiritual song.

Coffee was the one drink which Fred simply could not survive without.

August 7, 1973

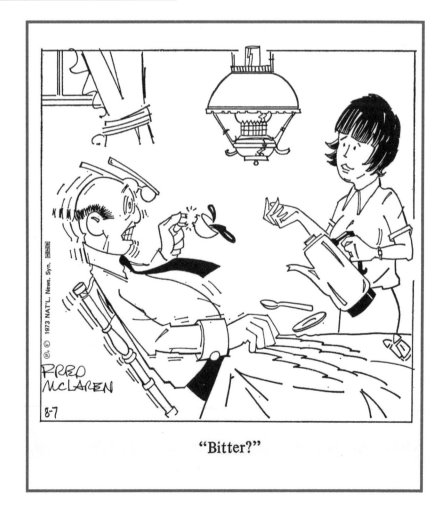

"Bitter?"

"I think old Thornsby has won the latest discussion over rock music!"

August 8, 1973

Fred often made fun of the United States Postal Service, based on his own personal experiences with delayed, lost, and mangled packages.

August 9, 1973

"Congratulations! All the way across town in only 17 days!"

"When did we ask to join an encounter group?"

August 10, 1973

'Touchy-feely' encounter groups that focused on interpersonal relations and self-understanding were very popular in the 1960s and 1970s.

August 11, 1973

"No, no, no! The fork goes on the left!"

August 13, 1973

"I don't want bow ties to come back—they make me look fat!"

Fred had a real-life fear of flying and only flew when absolutely necessary.

August 14, 1973

"On your left is Lake Michigan, on your right, at the tip of the wing, is your pilot making repairs."

"Hey man, Big Daddy here needs a fix!"

August 15, 1973

One of a small number of captions with Tune-In doing the talking, here in typical 1970s vernacular.

August 16, 1973

"Sure the rules are still the same: no grownups!"

August 17, 1973

"It's one of those novels that probes deep psychological motivations. As a matter of fact, it's filthy!"

Hoagy Carmichael's recording of the 1927 popular song "Stardust" became an American standard.

August 18, 1973

"It was a nice idea, Hon, but I think that's as close as they can ever come to 'Stardust.'"

"Of course you **know** those dents were on it **before** you brought it in!"

August 20, 1973

Fred once said if he were an actor, he would love to play a character with a snobbish attitude.

August 21, 1973

"...and would you care for a wine you can't pronounce from a year you know nothing about?"

"If I get any calls, just tell 'em I'm busy restoring my Duesenberg!"

August 22, 1973

One of Fred's weekend hobbies was building classic model cars.

The Thornsby plaid clearly pays homage to the Scottish roots of the MacLaren tartan.

August 23, 1973

"Oh, stop staring. You know perfectly well that's not the Thornsby plaid!"

August 24, 1973

"When you're done with your hair spray and hot comb, don't forget your mascara!"

August 25, 1973

"Zap! You're liberated! Now do the dishes."

August 27, 1973

" . . . Good news: I was cut from football and my roommate thinks she's pregnant, but I squeaked a 'D' in chemistry!"

One of the most detailed Thornsby comics, showing many of Fred's personal favorites from his youth.

August 28, 1973

"Control yourself, Dear."

August 29, 1973

"Only **my** husband has baby pictures that look like they were taken five minutes ago."

Hippie communes in the 1970s were known for rather rustic living conditions.

August 30, 1973

"Just a photo of the commune where I stayed last weekend."

August 31, 1973

"It's wonderful to talk to someone who can give the 'Now Generation' the perspective of old age!"

September 1, 1973

"One thing about Saturdays—it's always quiet downtown."

September 3, 1973

Many aging rockers suffer from hearing loss, including Eric Clapton, Pete Townshend, Roger Daltrey, Neil Young, Ozzy Osbourne, etc.

September 4, 1973

"I said: Doctors have proven that loud acid rock can cause hearing problems."

"Middle age is a time of subtle change. But in your case it's as subtle as a Sherman tank!"

September 5, 1973

Sherman tanks were first manufactured during World War II and became the prototype for future tank destroyers.

Platform shoes for men were a 1970s fad that continued into the disco era.

September 6, 1973

"You'll have to excuse my son. He's just learning to walk in high heels."

"What I'd really like is a hamburger
and french fries."

September 7, 1973

Fred's son Tom always ordered a
hamburger and french fries at
every restaurant he visited during
his childhood years.

September 8, 1973

"Well, we've had it for two weeks. Do you think
we can teach it to roll over and play dead?"

September 10, 1973

"IT'S CALLED THE NATURAL LOOK."

September 11, 1973

"I've decided to take up karate. After all, you're only young once!"

September 12, 1973

"Don't be nervous. The only difference between this and any other needle is a length of about three feet."

Artistic license: Tune-In's hair grew back the very next day!

September 13, 1973

"That haircut was too much of a shock for her. She hasn't seen your eyes for five years!"

September 14, 1973

"Welcome to Thornsby's Rest Home."

September 15, 1973

"Sometimes when I talk about my problems,
I feel I'm boring people to death!"

September 17, 1973

"Why am I being punished? My kid smokes pot, my wife reads Ms. Magazine, and I gain weight on diet cola !"

Fred actively collected pulp magazines and Big Little Books throughout his entire life. Both print formats were discontinued by the 1960s. Comic books have survived to current days.

September 18, 1973

"...had a lovely day housecleaning: threw out all those pulp magazines, comics, and Big Little Books you had stashed in the attic..."

September 19, 1973

"I seriously doubt, sir, that it would make an appropriate centerfold!"

September 20, 1973

"Well now...one for "uppers," one for "downers" and one for another hopeless attack on your waistline!"

September 21, 1973

"Remember the good old days when we could send him away to camp?"

September 22, 1973

"O.K. You're not conservative, you're not liberal. But you've got to be for <u>something</u>. You can't just be for nostalgia!"

"Where are Doris Day and Pat Boone
now that we need them?"

September 24, 1973

When the Hays Code was
removed by the Motion Picture
Association of America in 1966,
wholesome movies starring Doris
Day and Pat Boone quickly
disappeared from mainstream
cinema.

September 25, 1973

"I know you like to jog around after work,
Dear. But you're late for supper!"

September 26, 1973

"Look in here. A perfect example of poor oral hygiene---too much smoking, too many sweets. Get the ax!"

Fred never wore bow ties, white shoes, or suspenders.

September 27, 1973

"Bow ties are back, white shoes are back. But _those_ are never coming back !"

"Comfy?"

September 28, 1973

Fred developed a fear of heights, which increased as he aged. In the 1960s however, he did (safely) climb onto the roof to paint the ridge and eaves of the family home.

September 29, 1973

"Don't blame me! YOU gave him a drum when he was four so he could be 'creative!'"

October 1, 1973

"Well, Mr. Success has made it through another Monday!"

Pornography and obscenity issues were actively debated in the Supreme Court throughout the 1960s and 1970s.

October 2, 1973

"Listen, Bud, ya want real power? I've got magazines that'll let ya defy the Supreme Court!"

October 3, 1973

"Men! Are you bald, overweight,
grumpy, nearsighted, run-down,
and unable to cope?"

In this era, network television
banned commercials showing
models wearing brassieres and
other underwear.

October 4, 1973

"...and notice how 'Gorgeous Bra'
holds, lifts and allures..."

"...After our new car broke down I was late for the 9:00 meeting and couldn't find my notes and didn't have time for coffee and..."

October 5, 1973

Adding visual humor, Tune-In is 'playing the violin' in a show of faux sympathy.

October 6, 1973

"We just had a long talk about the generation gap...I said 'hello' and he said 'see ya'!"

October 8, 1973

A single-panel comic occasionally limits a cartoonist's creativity, so in a few instances Fred would expand Thornsby into multiple panels filling a square single-panel space.

October 9, 1973

141

"How's <u>that</u> for volume?"

October 10, 1973

October 11, 1973

"Sorry, she can't see anyone now--she's posing for a Playboy centerfold!"

"You don't understand--she's only my roommate until midnight weekdays and until 2 a.m. weekends. We've got rules!"

October 12, 1973

Tune-In and Vibes were examples of the younger generation's philosophy of free love.

October 13, 1973

"Long hair, pony tail, high heels, hip-huggers, hand bags--let's change his name to Linda!"

October 15, 1973

October 16, 1973

"If they'd dressed like that when <u>we</u> were in college, they would have <u>had</u> us in an intensive care unit!"

October 17, 1973

"They've been getting along very well--
some days for two or three minutes
at a time!"

October 18, 1973

"At the office Thornsby is just sort
of dull and middle-aged, but at a
party he's a real bore!"

"Here's Thornsby. That strike zone will give you fits!"

October 19, 1973

Fred was a devoted Chicago Cubs fan his entire life. The McLarens frequently went to Wrigley Field in the late 60s and early 70s to see afternoon games. Fred's last visit to Wrigley was in 2011 for an insider tour of the stadium.

Blanch's silhouette was accomplished through the use of Zip-A-Tone screentone paper. Fred frequently used Zip-A-Tone to establish a gray coloring effect.

October 20, 1973

"The 'Miss Nude America' title is safe!"

"And I was fined $10
for burning leaves!"

October 22, 1973

Pollution and smog reached a dangerous peak in the 1970s, leading to the creation of the EPA. Note the masks worn by the background characters - who knew then that the COVID-19 scare of 2020 would reach worldwide pandemic proportions (with everyone wearing masks everywhere)?

October 23, 1973

"Never mind the long lost relatives
bit. Just help me contact 1973!"

October 24, 1973

"I'm sure there's a melody in there someplace, but they'll never find it!"

October 25, 1973

"Nobody's trying to weaken your will power. I was just in the mood for homemade bread, pies, cakes, cookies.."

"Here's that <u>terrible</u> scene again: I hate it! Hate it so much I've been back four times!"

October 26, 1973

It seemed that almost every movie in the 1970s had some form of nudity on the big screen.

October 27, 1973

"He's finally grown up, after smoking pot, joining a rock group and flunking college. Now he's 'involved'!"

October 29, 1973

"You'll never dig my scene, Pops. I mean, can you just imagine yourself...   ...with long hair?"

October 30, 1973

"Trick or Treat! What a bore! When we were kids we played some real pranks on grownups!"

"Talk about sentimentalists! He'll risk a fine just so 'October smells like October'!"

October 31, 1973

Fred loved the fall season, with all its sentimental sights, sounds, and smells. Bans of leaf burning started in the late 1960s.

The Battle of the Sexes with chauvinistic Bobby Riggs vs. triumphant Billie Jean King was a pop culture event in 1973.

November 1, 1973

"The rise and fall of male chauvinism!"

November 2, 1973

'Handy Andy' strikes again!

November 3, 1973

"Pick up: 11 a.m. and 2 p.m., alternate
Wednesdays (when convenient). Not
responsible for delivery."

November 5, 1973

Thornsby's spare tire was the butt of many jokes (no pun intended) - in this case, a perfect tie-in to the Firestone Tire and Rubber Company.

November 6, 1973

"Thornsby, you could make a fortune!
Just have 'Firestone' printed across
there!"

"Watch this one, Marlon--it's glass!"

November 7, 1973

Bad experiences from the McLaren family's move in the summer of 1973 led to many comics lampooning careless moving company employees.

November 8, 1973

"They all go back to cigarettes sooner or later!"

"Nice going, Pierre! Maybe I can hold supper....while we wait another four weeks for steaks!"

November 9, 1973

The meat shortage of 1973 was an unusual crisis at the time (and a big problem for meat-and-potatoes Midwestern families, like the McLarens).

In the background of this cartoon, an X-rated movie theatre has a 'closed' sign. With the success of the infamous pornographic film "Deep Throat" in 1972, first amendment rights were hotly debated in local communities everywhere.

November 10, 1973

"You can't tell me she meets 'acceptable local community standards'!"

November 12, 1973

"Take heart, Hon. Monday
comes but once a week!"

November 13, 1973

"Oh, now I see--we were supposed to
pull the ones on the right side!"

"Would you believe she was once a
Sunday school teacher in Ellison
Bay, Wisconsin?"

November 14, 1973

In the late 1960s, the McLaren
family vacationed in Ellison Bay,
Wisconsin. This tiny town is a
well-known retreat or artists and
other creative people.

The 1970s energy crisis wreaked
havoc on the Western world.
Gasoline rationing, long lines at
gas stations, and reduced speed
limits became the norm.

November 15, 1973

"It's no use, mister. Besides, I don't
want 43 World War II comic books!"

"Charlie's been an old friend and mascot around here...Still, if the price were right...."

November 16, 1973

Tommy Dorsey was another one of Fred's big band era favorites. The Rainbow Room at the top of Rockefeller Center was a world famous restaurant and nightclub (and is now a private event space). Fred saw Duke Ellington perform there in the 1960s.

November 17, 1973

"It's just not the same place without Tommy Dorsey!"

"Right now I'm witness to the total breakdown of the intel lectual community."

November 19, 1973

Although Fred loved big band music, he did not like the wholesome sounds of Lawrence Welk. The McLaren household never watched his long-running TV series.

Fred was a big fan of "Ellery Queen's Mystery Magazine" and other similar fiction publications that featured short stories.

November 20, 1973

"Somewhere in there is a magazine with an old-fashioned mystery short story!"

"Nader's right! Nothing's made
to work right anymore!"

November 21, 1973

Consumer advocate Ralph Nader
was such a household name at
that time, Fred didn't need to use
his first name in the caption.

November 22, 1973

"They've closed my
X-rated moviehouse,
adult bookstore and
underground newstand...

..but I've got some
great shots of my
old customers!"

"The girls demand equal pay, the drivers want shorter hours, and Thornsby wants time off for 'an important Superman film festival.'"

November 23, 1973

Look very closely in the upper left corner for the 'New Lenox Line' truck, a reference to the McLaren's hometown from 1961 to 1973.

November 24, 1973

"I get the feeling we're not wanted out here."

November 26, 1973

"All right! <u>All</u> <u>right</u>! I'll wear something conservative."

November 27, 1973

"Behind every successful man, there's a moody, unpredictable, and slightly overweight lady who..."

November 28, 1973

"When I was in college, MY roomate was a fat football player with an I.Q. of 89 and a bad case of acne!"

Fred and Thornsby loved to poke fun at the younger generation's different forms of rebellion.

November 29, 1973

"You see, They just can't stand conformity."

November 30, 1973

"Those magazines constitute the cheapest kind of exploitation! Besides that, they're irresistable!"

Thornsby's father made a few appearances, showing the family's genetic predisposition towards hair loss and poor eyesight.

Note the cane on the left with the Thornsby handle.

December 1, 1973

"Do as I've done son. Learn to change with the times."

December 3, 1973

"After a hard day, he just counts his
hang-ups until he falls asleep!"

December 4, 1973

"So remember: sell your papers, save
your money, stay in school, go to
church, and GET THAT HAIR CUT!"

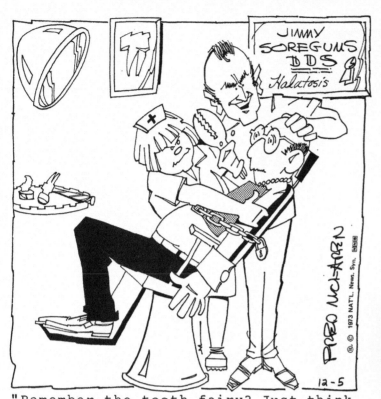

December 5, 1973

"Remember the tooth fairy? Just think, tonight you can put all 32 of those under your pillow at one time!"

December 6, 1973

"If that's the road to inner peace, let's give thanks for ulcers and high blood pressure."

December 7, 1973

"'An accelerated spare tire' in medical terms means that someday there's going to be this giant explosion..."

The Red Ryder BB gun was introduced in the 1930s and later immortalized in the 1983 classic movie "A Christmas Story."

December 8, 1973

"The city may be more dangerous, but nobody will be frightened by your old 'Red Ryder' BB gun!"

"Forget it, dearheart!"

December 10, 1973

Introduced in June 1973, "Playgirl" was the first publication aimed at women to regularly feature male nudity.

Fred's caricature is featured on the newspaper Thornsby is holding.

December 11, 1973

"Willie, I think you're putting me on!"

"Around here we have 10 minutes of dead silence after he reads the news!"

December 12, 1973

For those who thought college tuition was expensive in the 1970s, it was just the beginning of the skyrocketing cost of education.

December 13, 1973

"About these expenses: It was tough getting him into college, but how can we get him to drop out?"

December 14, 1973

"Molle Mystery Theatre" was a radio show from 1943-1948, later renamed "CBS Mystery Theatre" from 1948-1951.

A 1940s (before) and 1970s (after) version of Thornsby and a kindly store owner.

December 15, 1973

December 17, 1973

"What I really enjoy about winter is getting up on Monday mornings...

... Finding the car won't start, and waiting hours for a bus that's probably been recalled!"

"Thrilling Detective" was a popular pulp magazine from the 1930s - 1950s.

Note the witty nameplate for this loan company employee: N.O. Empathy.

December 18, 1973

"I can't believe you seriously thought we'd accept as collateral a complete run of 'Thrilling Detective'!"

"Oh help! It's time for another rustic evening by the fire!"

December 19, 1973

Fred loved wood-burning fireplaces like the one in the family's London, Ontario home, despite the occasional mishap (who forgot to open the flue?).

December 20, 1973

"Aw-- Did your poor little baby catch cold?"

December 21, 1973

"**Now** they've gone too far!"

The Christmas window displays at Marshall Field's in downtown Chicago were a treat for the entire McLaren family.

Fred also loved the allure of an old-fashioned sleeper train with a dining car.

December 22, 1973

"Those great old passenger trains are still running, dear- if only in the windows."

December 24, 1973

"Don't look at me -- I've never had the heart to tell him!"

December 25, 1973

"Gee, just what I wanted -- the complete recordings of The Rolling Stones."

"You'll be happy to know we had a traditional Christmas here at college -- 24 girls visited the frat house for a 5-day bash!"

December 26, 1973

December 27, 1973

"This is an emergency: The world's greatest do-it-yourselfer just re-wired the whole house for stereo!"

December 28, 1973

"Want to drive him crazy? Ask about the time he tried out for 'the thin man' in the school play!"

December 29, 1973

"My, my. Fame at last!"

December 31, 1973

"What do you mean 'grubby'? Everyone dresses up for New Year's Eve!"

January 1, 1974

"We here at sports control hope this bright, sunny New Year's morning is a happy one for you..."

January 2, 1974

"Check this: '1974 women's lib convention to be held on Isle of Man'! Maybe they'll get lucky and find one!"

January 3, 1974

"Now that's 'body language' -- she's trying to tell me I'm still young and handsome!"

January 4, 1974

The marriage counselor Dr. Pink n' Wiggly was a one-time guest character. Blanch is not going to tolerate Thornsby's obvious interest.

"Now I'm sure we don't need 'professional help'!"

Fred smoked Lucky Strike cigarettes for many years and saved an original Flat Fifties tin, which he kept on display in all his residences.

January 5, 1974

"You're misunderstood? Listen, I once had my allowance cut for carrying a pack of Luckies!"

"His big problem is background -- in college his major was <u>conservative</u> arts!"

January 7, 1974

Food for thought for those who have wondered why the traditional academic program in most universities is named Liberal Arts.

Cass Elliott was a talented singer (best known for being a member of the Mamas and the Papas) who passed away a few months after this comic was published.

January 8, 1974

"Let's put him on the scales and let him do his Mama Cass imitation!"

"Well, it's sure not a revival of 'Woman's Home Companion'!"

January 9, 1974

"Viva" was an adult women's magazine in the 1970s, similar to "Playgirl" magazine.

What's in your flooded basement? All collectors like Fred and son Tom know to never store anything in a basement unless it's protected by sealed plastic wrap!

January 10, 1974

"Well, you never kept anything down here except junk, anyway!"

"Thornsby!"

January 11, 1974

The St. Louis Post-Dispatch refused to run this comic, likely because strippers were too risqué. The newspaper ran a previously published comic instead.

Fred saved a set of first edition books from author Edgar Allan Poe.

January 12, 1974

"She may remind you of 1945, but she reminds me of Edgar Allen Poe!"

January 14, 1974

"You win. I could've sworn the girl was the one on the right!"

January 15, 1974

"Heard the latest? They say pot smoking will make your hair fall out!"

"Say! Isn't that the original 1935 Tom Mix six-shooter? I'll give you $25.00 for it!"

"Geez-ya meet some real nuts in this business!"

January 16, 1974

Tom Mix was a popular film and radio actor in Westerns from the 1910s to the 1930s. A six-shooter toy gun was marketed to children of that era.

James 'you dirty, yellow-bellied rat' Cagney was best known for his gangster movies, which were considered violent during the 1930s and 1940s.

January 17, 1974

"I can remember when we thought James Cagney was too violent!"

January 18, 1974

"Timing is the thing -- when he's completely out of gas, I'll hit him for a fast 20 bucks!"

January 19, 1974

"The anesthesia's wearing off. We'll flip to see who tells him we took out his tonsils by mistake!"

"O.K. I'm patriotic.
I turned down the
thermostat..."

...Now I can lay awake
all night and listen to the
plumbing freeze solid!"

January 21, 1974

In response to the energy crisis, President Nixon asked Americans to lower their thermostats to 68 degrees during the winter months.

Big band swing musician Glenn Miller was the best-selling recording artist from 1939-1942.

January 22, 1974

"Stop clowning! You'll never get his attention while he's listening to Glenn Miller!"

"Blanch -- do I have the wrong priorities in life?"

"Why no. You're right in step with the 40's!"

January 23, 1974

January 24, 1974

"You're uptight.   Go home, read two episodes in 'Heros Comics,' and give me a call in the morning!"

January 25, 1974

"Boy I wish I were 25 years younger...

...I was really dashing in those days!"

January 26, 1974

"I can say this about my dad: He's hip! Really with it! I can say this 'cause I'm half smashed!"

"Remember, it's Monday. Don't say a word to him 'til he's had his third cup!"

January 28, 1974

Thornsby's newspaper features a drawing of Nixon and reports a long list of shortages (based on real life events in 1973-74).

Popular singer Johnny Cash did a memorable TV commercial in 1973 promoting energy conservation.

January 29, 1974

"I don't care what Johnny Cash says! Let's at least light another candle!"

January 30, 1974

"If this is the first day of the rest of my life, why start it off with your coffee?"

Fred never changed his hairstyle. He didn't embrace the creativity of men's salons (in this cartoon, stylist Peter Pamper offered Shirley Temple cuts for men).

January 31, 1974

"40 years ago he was the neighborhood terror. Now he looks just like my aunt Maud!"

"Don't wake her. She's building her case for equal pay!"

February 1, 1974

The gender wage gap exploded in the 1970s as women demanded equal pay and brought sex-discrimination suits to court.

The cigarette pack on the woman's desk is branded 'Tar & Goo' and the magazine is named 'I'll Confess to Anything.'

February 2, 1974

"If they really are 'conservation freaks', why don't they turn off those electric guitars!"

February 4, 1974

The World Food Crisis of 1972-1975 is traced back to shortages in the international grain markets and famines in several foreign countries.

February 5, 1974

"...I'll go over it again. After the 'coaltruck' dumped it into a 'coalbin' you'd pour it into a 'stoker'."

February 6, 1974

Fred loved the mystique of steam locomotives. The 1974 version of "Murder on the Orient Express" was one of his favorite contemporary films, because the train was "one of the stars."

February 7, 1974

"Be right with you Thornsby...Soon as Rancid rounds up a few more tools!"

February 8, 1974

"Let's see: YES, he's republican, NO, he's against rationing, and YES, he's for women's lib!"

February 9, 1974

"I may not know a 'bummer' from a 'ripoff', but I do know the smell of 'pot'!"

February 11, 1974

"Captain Midnight" was a radio serial, which originally ran from 1938 to 1949. One of Fred's prized collectibles was a Captain Midnight Secret Squadron badge.

"I can tell you this much -- There were no hi-jackers when Captain Midnight was around!"

February 12, 1974

"Your center of gravity wasn't made for those heels!"

February 13, 1974

"A sure cure: 3 tablets every 4 hours, 4 pills every 3 hours, 2 teaspoons every 12 hours and $10 to me every 24 hours!"

The oil embargo of 1973 caused gasoline supplies to dwindle and prices to soar.

The address of Ye Olde Gift Shop is 20 N. Wacker (the actual Chicago address of Thornsby syndicator National Newspaper Syndicate).

February 14, 1974

February 15, 1974

"Just leave him alone! You KNOW if either one of us had any hair left, we'd let it grow!"

February 16, 1974

"It's all your fault. You called it sloppy and hurt its feelings!"

February 18, 1974

"I never think about them anymore. I quit
3 months, 2 days, 11 hours and 34 seconds ago!"

The St. Louis Post-Dispatch
replaced this cartoon with a
previously published one. The
marijuana theme was apparently
too hot to handle, though this was
not the first Thornsby comic to
reference pot.

February 19, 1974

"I was only kidding about the pot shortage!"

"Dear, I hope you didn't expect a big turnout."

February 20, 1974

"Terry and the Pirates" was a newspaper comic strip which ran for almost 40 years. Fred was unhappy when it was discontinued in 1973.

Thornsby is giving his late night excuse his best shot i.e. giving it the old college try.

February 21, 1974

"Your story lacks credibility. But you do win the Richard Nixon 'college try' contest!"

"Goodness! Another 17 inches expected tonight!"

February 22, 1974

Fred always lived in the Midwest, so shoveling snow was a chore to look forward to every winter season.

February 23, 1974

"Not another fad diet!"

February 25, 1974

"Boy! 2 more weeks on my diet and they'll
want me on the cover of 'Playgirl'!"

February 26, 1974

"Brakes, steering and suspension! By the time they
recall my new car, it'll be too old to trade in!"

February 27, 1974

"Maybe I should try that hot comb. I just washed
my hair, and can't do a thing with it!"

'The Petty Girl' was a series of
sexy pin-up paintings by George
Petty from the 1930s-1950s. The
pin-ups were popular 'nose art' on
airplanes during World War II.

February 28, 1974

"What's he know? He thought the Petty girl
was hot stuff!"

March 1, 1974

"For crying out loud! It's 3 o'clock in the morning. Nobody is going to see you!"

March 2, 1974

"... and then she has to say: 'It wasn't funny when you ran out of gas 30 years ago either!' "

"Now I'm ready to close the generation gap!"

March 4, 1974

Fred grew a mustache in the 1980s, which he kept for the remainder of his life - but he never grew a beard.

Fred of course included himself in the background as one of the nostalgia buffs.

March 5, 1974

"Oh, it's a bargain all right. 25 years ago you paid 25¢ for it, and now it's $25!"

March 6, 1974

"And to think when I was a kid, I used to walk out on love scenes!"

March 7, 1974

"It's the return of the abdominal snowman!"

"Now this is what I call planned obsolescence.
Every year he trades it in for a new model!"

March 8, 1974

Styles didn't change as fast as Thornsby predicted, but wide ties and long hair for men were a 1970s trend. One sure thing we can all count on with fashion and style: everything old is new again.

March 9, 1974

" Just wait. Thin ties, short hair, and white
shirts will be back this spring!"

"Neither rain, nor snow, nor gloom of night prevents him from running around like an idiot!"

March 11, 1974

Boosted by the 1972 Summer Olympics, jogging and running became a national pastime for millions of Americans in the 70s.

March 12, 1974

"Gee, I never thought I'd welcome a power failure!"

March 13, 1974

The 1970s bicycle boom was fitting for those who wanted recreation, exercise, reduced pollution, and an inexpensive method of commuting to work.

"Forget it, hon. Maybe you can find a car pool."

March 14, 1974

"Hey man, we've got to know where you get your Afro done!"

"There's not a word in here about the king being more important than the queen!"

March 15, 1974

Chess is the only board game which Fred played during his adult years. A handmade wood chess board was always set up and ready for play in his various homes.

March 16, 1974

"College hasn't changed, dad. My roomate and I will be studying all night for exams!"

March 18, 1974

"Don't be smug about it, son. Mine's
a natural too!"

March 19, 1974

"This is 'dial-nostalgia'. Today you will hear a
model T engine that ran 33 years without a recall."

"Now can we throw away the Dr. Spock books?"

March 20, 1974

Dr. Spock's book "The Common Sense Book of Baby and Child Care" is considered by many to be the definitive guide for raising children. The book has sold more than 50 million copies worldwide.

Fred always preferred button-down collared shirts for business and casual wear. He never wore t-shirts in public.

March 21, 1974

"I'm not saying you're square, hon. But just once, wear a colored shirt to the office!"

"You're overreacting! Just because C.B.S. radio has brought back 'mystery theater'..."

March 22, 1974

A nostalgic throwback to the golden age of radio, the "CBS Radio Mystery Theatre" was broadcast from 1974 to 1982.

The feature film "The Exorcist" was released in December 1973 and became a massive hit. Exorcism terminology quickly became part of the world's vocabulary.

March 23, 1974

"It's exorcism! Blanch shows him a lawnmower, and he gets the devil out of there!"

March 25, 1974

"Listen! Anyone who calls his return a 'game plan', is automatically suspect!"

March 26, 1974

"Mother? Now there's another crisis. They've ex-changed gift certificates for Harry's Barber Shop!"

March 27, 1974

"Well, there goes the ol' neighborhood!"

March 28, 1974

"I can't sleep! Somewhere, someone has his thermostat turned up to 74!"

March 29, 1974

"I'm not a sexist, but I certainly understand the male mystique!"

March 30, 1974

"I don't know what it is, but I've got the title: 'Thornsby Gropes Again'!"

"Nice idea, Thornsby, but this just wasn't made for a car pool!"

April 1, 1974

See if you can spot President Nixon, Sherlock Holmes, and W.C. Fields in this car pool.

Thornsby is reading "Action Comics" issue #1, which marked the first appearance of Superman. A pristine copy of this June 1938 comic sold on eBay for a record $3.2 million.

April 2, 1974

"I'm not living in the past! I'm a serious student of cultural change and historical trends!"

April 3, 1974

"Good heavens! That's not the way he said
grace before he went off to college!"

April 4, 1974

"Your test results are back Thornsby, and...well,
I want to wish you all the luck in the world!"

April 5, 1974

"I'll bet you didn't get the raise either!"

April 6, 1974

"This spring I think it's going to take more than baseball to get him out of the house!"

April 8, 1974

"Like he says: 'Once you know how, you never forget'!"

Thornsby's wall is filled with references to Fred's personal life, including the license plates 485-6869 (Fred's phone number in New Lenox, Illinois) and 472-5122 (Fred's phone number in London, Ontario).

April 9, 1974

"And you're always bugging me about keeping my room clean!"

"But will your son really like 312 recordings
by Sammy Kaye?"

April 10, 1974

Sammy Kaye is another popular
big band leader with a huge
catalog of vintage recordings.

April 11, 1974

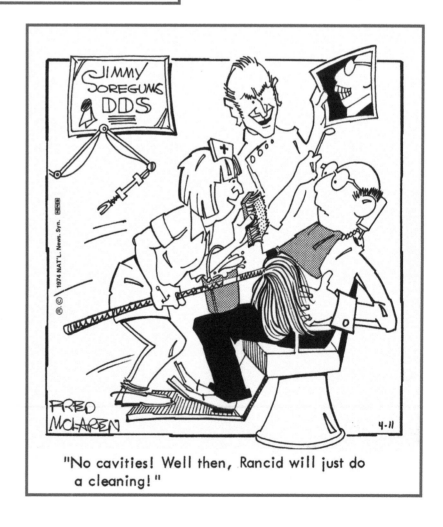

"No cavities! Well then, Rancid will just do
a cleaning!"

April 12, 1974

"You must be losing weight! It only took you 7 minutes getting your socks on this morning!"

April 13, 1974

"Gee, here it is Easter weekend, and we're already getting last year's Christmas cards!"

"I'm surprised, son. I thought you wide-eyed
conservationists were all for 'dialing down'!"

April 15, 1974

Pollution and anti-smoking
protests begged for clean air
everywhere. Congress banned
cigarette advertisements on
television and radio beginning
January 2, 1971.

April 16, 1974

"It's a good cause. Let's donate a bar of soap
to each one!"

April 17, 1974

The streaking phenomenon peaked in the mid-1970s as college students everywhere stripped down for laughs and shock value.

"If your son insists on 'streaking', why does he have to stay in my neighborhood?"

The St. Louis Post-Dispatch banished this comic as well, clearly because the woman's tight sweater makes her appear topless.

April 18, 1974

"For Mr. Thornsby I don't type, take dictation, answer the phone or make coffee. I just breathe!"

April 19, 1974

Oversized black velvet bow ties were a trendy fashion statement at this time.

"I knew one of these new velvet jobs would take off about 20 years!"

Inspiration for this comic: Fred's wife Betty Lou was terrified of dogs, because of an incident during her youth.

April 20, 1974

"It's O.K. big fella. One meal at our house and you'd be afraid of her!"

April 22, 1974

April 23, 1974

"Is it a 'streaker'? Is it a 'jogger'? No! It's 'super waddler'!"

April 24, 1974

Fred didn't practice yoga, so the moaning associated with mantra chanting was something he never understood.

April 25, 1974

"Are you sure it's yoga? Maybe all they need is a giant bottle of Pepto-Bismol!"

"'Respect', he sez. So I sez:'Listen fella, we treat all our cars with care and respect!'"

April 26, 1974

Fred was very hesitant to trust any garage mechanic with the care and handling of his prized Morgan sports car.

Launched in 1926, Old Gold cigarettes had a long-running marketing campaign with the slogan 'not a cough in a carload.'

April 27, 1974

"Before he quit, he claimed that there wasn't 'a cough in a carload'!"

"The book says 'I'm O.K. – You're O.K.' – but he got it wrong. He's been K.O.'d for years!"

April 29, 1974

"I'm OK - You're OK" was a popular self-help book by Thomas Anthony Harris, first published in 1967.

April 30, 1974

"Take what you need, Mister. But touch those 'Big Little Books', and I'll break your neck!"

"Y'know, I think it would be more appropriate if you wore a mask!"

May 1, 1974

Inflation ran rampant in the 1970s and became an everyday struggle for all families. The Great Inflation period lasted from 1965 to 1982.

May 2, 1974

"... and shall we thin it out on top?"

May 3, 1974

"Oh! Home movies of your Florida trip! We'd
love to come over and see them!"

May 4, 1974

"No kidding! You mean he was once just a
97 lb. weakling?"

"I'm breaking out of this routine, and I'm going to do something wild! Like missing the 8:07!"

May 6, 1974

During his commercial art years in the 1960s and early 1970s, Fred commuted by train from New Lenox to Chicago every work day.

New Lenox was pleasant, but Illinois had dreary suburbs as well (which served as inspiration for Thornsby's Sludgeville).

Fred's sons Tom and Fred were Cub Scouts and Boy Scouts during their childhood years in New Lenox, Illinois.

May 7, 1974

"Just think-- four years ago today he made eagle scout!"

"'In sickness and in health' ... as long as he
doesn't catch anything!"

May 8, 1974

Fred was an extreme germophobe
and this scenario was more truth
than fiction in the McLaren
household.

May 9, 1974

"Don't yell at me. He's the one who said
'Try to pass those dummies'!"

"Don't be silly. Julie Eisenhower would never run off with John Dean!"

May 10, 1974

Thornsby was always tied to contemporary events and people: Julie Eisenhower is President Nixon's daughter and John Dean is a former attorney who served as White House Counsel during the Watergate years.

The Guru movement became very popular in the United States during the late 1960s and 1970s.

May 11, 1974

"Get some rest, watch your weight and don't take Ralph Nadar seriously."

May 13, 1974

"Oh dear. Now I suppose I'll have to listen to how your day went."

May 14, 1974

"I told you they'd never buy that weekend in Dallas on the ol' expense account!"

May 15, 1974

May 16, 1974

"What cracks me up is that Blanch thinks
I'm at a baseball game!"

May 17, 1974

In 1974 Sister Janet Mead scored a Top 10 international hit single with a soft rock version of "The Lord's Prayer."

May 18, 1974

"I don't think they're ready for a rock version
of 'The Lord's Prayer'!"

May 20, 1974

"It's old hat now, but if <u>you</u> were to try it..."

Formal impeachment hearings against President Nixon began May 9, 1974 - just 12 days before this comic was published.

Fun family fact: the lamp in this comic is a replica of Fred's favorite lamp (which son Tom still uses to this very day).

May 21, 1974

"Oh, stop it! I voted for him too, y'know!"

May 22, 1974

"Oh, go ahead and buy one. She never comes
in here!"

May 23, 1974

May 24, 1974

"I don't know about this mod outfit- the girls at the office may have trouble controlling themselves!"

May 25, 1974

"After her weekend away, I'll bet your mother will be glad to get home!"

May 27, 1974

"You never talk to me like that anymore!"

May 28, 1974

"Now I remember: we piled up all those savings bonds so he could go to college and 'adjust' to a roomate!"

"We acknowledge the 1937 geog. papers donated to the Lib. of Congress, but you still owe us $47.17."

May 29, 1974

Look closely to see the IRS envelope on the kitchen table. Thornsby (and Fred) never enjoyed paying taxes.

May 30, 1974

"I seem to be holding up very well. - It's that receding hairline that worries me!"

May 31, 1974

"Forget it fella– I just caught the news,
and now I'm depressed!"

The cities listed in this caption all
had newspapers which carried
Thornsby at this time.

June 1, 1974

"Let's see: Lincoln Neb., Buffalo N.Y., Detroit and
Chicago. Tell y'what–next time just send it direct!"

"Oh, he's still off cigarettes.
Now it's dime cigars!"

June 3, 1974

The first of many comics with a cigar smoking theme. Fred was primarily a cigarette smoker, but he smoked cigars for a short period during the Thornsby years, much to his family's dismay.

June 4, 1974

"It's amazing, dear, but you've actually stayed on your new diet for 24 hours!"

June 5, 1974

"He just loves those unrequested credit cards!"

June 6, 1974

"I'll try to be subtle- who's your next of kin?"

"Here's a killer: June, 1967– the last
time she tried a bikini."

June 7, 1974

Long before the digital age, Fred's
son Tom had a View-Master table-
top projector that displayed
images from a picture wheel.

June 8, 1974

"I'm impressed. Out here, over a campfire, your
coffee is just as rotten as back home!"

June 10, 1974

"Sorry I mentioned it: I didn't think you missed the great taste and aroma of cigarettes."

June 11, 1974

"Take two baths and call me in the morning."

June 12, 1974

The plain brown wrapper was used by the postal service to (discretely) deliver adult-oriented men's magazines.

"Five'll get you ten she came in a plain, brown wrapper!"

June 13, 1974

"Hi doc- how's the recession?"

June 14, 1974

"No dessert– he's cutting down!"

June 15, 1974

"If you insist on wearing your hair like a long-haired hippie, you can at least keep it neat!"

"For Father's Day he gave me 2 oz. of pot and a year's subscription to 'National Lampoon'."

June 17, 1974

"National Lampoon" magazine launched in 1970 and quickly became a pop culture brand in all forms of media.

June 18, 1974

"Listen— if I had had more than one, would I offer you excuse that accept you could of?"

"Now that I have everyone's attention..."

June 19, 1974

As men transitioned to longer hair styles in the 70s, barber shops declined in popularity when salons offered a greater variety of services for both men and women.

June 20, 1974

"You can't get a regular haircut anymore.
But how 'bout a unisex trim?"

"What this country needs is one more shortage—
CHEAP CIGARS!"

June 21, 1974

Smoke so thick 'you could cut it with a knife.' Reminiscent of the McLaren household at this time.

One of Fred's favorite stories: Debbie Reynolds said in an interview that she opened her refrigerator door late one night, the light shined on her, and she started performing her Vegas act.

June 22, 1974

"I know, I know, but he thinks it's Las Vegas
and there's a full house out there!"

June 24, 1974

"This must be his second or third Monday morning so far this week!"

June 25, 1974

"Dear -- we're just not communicating these days."

June 26, 1974

"Sure I like a cosmopolitan city, it's just that some days I feel like a token wasp!"

Factory seconds (aka factory rejects) are flawed retail items that are typically sold to the public at a reduced rate.

June 27, 1974

"It's unreal! You've lost 15 pounds and you still look like a factory second!"

June 28, 1974

"You talk to them! He told me it was research for 'Physiology II'!"

June 29, 1974

"Just ignore him. If you say anything he'll slow down!"

July 1, 1974

"Mother!"

July 2, 1974

"You're lookin' good. NOW exhale!"

July 3, 1974

July 4, 1974

"I slipped in an old Guy Lombardo record
just to see what'd happen!"

July 5, 1974

"And then you wrote, 'just think how romantic it'll be to be alone in our own little house'..."

The McLaren family lived in suburban London, Ontario in the mid-70s and encountered subdivision rules & regulations for the first time.

July 6, 1974

"Wait 'til they find out mine is 1/8" higher than theirs!"

"It's too bad Kissinger only goes after the big ones!"

July 8, 1974

Henry Kissinger was a controversial political figure, well known for his role in negotiating the ceasefire in Vietnam.

July 9, 1974

"We all have our little ways of learning to cope, dear!"

"If this causes headaches, nausea and sleeping sickness-- do let me know!"

July 10, 1974

Fred's original (discarded) hand-written caption for this comic was: "This might work. Or give you headaches, nausea, or the Aztec hops. Let me know how you make out!"

Henny Youngman was a comedian who was famous for telling one-liners ("Take my wife...please"), with violin in hand.

July 11, 1974

"First he just read to them, but now it's Henny Youngman time!"

"Pushover! Can't you tell he's too young to really remember 'Kraft Music Hall'?"

July 12, 1974

"Kraft Music Hall" was a popular radio variety show from 1933 to 1949. Various versions appeared on television starting in the late 1950s.

Fred's original handwritten caption was: "There's no end to all these funny cars - ours is the only garage in town to get pregnant every summer!"

July 13, 1974

"It's as if our garage gets pregnant every summer!"

July 15, 1974

"Forget it! I can't relate
to chubby ones."

July 16, 1974

"Goodness! I'll bet you forgot to stop
by the store on your way home, too!"

"What do you mean 'sexist'?"

July 17, 1974

Fred's original handwritten caption was from Blanch's point of view: "Where DO you get this sexist stuff?"

Paul Whiteman was referred to as 'The King of Jazz' during the 1920s. His heyday was before Fred's time, but Whiteman remained a popular musician, particularly in radio, through the 1950s.

July 18, 1974

"Sure, I've got blue chips- you should see my Paul Whiteman collection!"

July 19, 1974

"There! You see- you're not listening!"

July 20, 1974

"Hide your children-- here's Miss August playmate!"

"This isn't going to look good
on your resume!"

July 22, 1974

Thornsby's boss was originally
Gordon Darwin, but was replaced
by Grim Snorbart in later comics.

Fred's original handwritten
caption was: "Monday morning or
no Monday morning, this isn't
going to look good on your
resume!"

July 23, 1974

"Before I came here I was
a food junkie!"

July 24, 1974

Chess aficionados will remember a classic 1919 match with Jose Raul Capablanca defeating Borislav Kostic.

"Based on Capablanca vs. Kostic, I'd say your 1st move was a big mistake!"

Sexual freedom exploded in the 1970s, with swinging (and phrases like 'wife-swapping' and 'key parties') arriving in Middle America.

July 25, 1974

"Dear, it's been a long time since 'swinging' referred to dance music!"

July 26, 1974

In suburbia and at public parks, the joys of picnicking outside are often canceled out by the birds.

"It's just a friendly game of 'gotcha'!"

The 1970s 'Keep America Beautiful' campaign was heavily criticized for deflecting responsibility away from major beverage and packaging corporations.

July 27, 1974

"I loved their T.V. commercial about: 'Concern for our environment'!"

"20 years ago she would have
brought out the riot squad!"

July 29, 1974

Fred's original handwritten
caption was: "Imagine this
comin' down the street 20 years
ago - and in the background, the
sirens of the riot squad!"

Marijuana was a frequent theme,
but this is the only Thornsby
comic to reference hard drugs.

July 30, 1974

"O.K. I know all
about acid rock
and hard rock...

But you can't tell me
mainlining has nothing
to do with railroads!"

July 31, 1974

"It's acute indigestion... bring in the Richter scale!"

August 1, 1974

"Slow down and you'll go to bed without your supper!"

"Well, there are exceptions!"

August 2, 1974

August 3, 1974

"Well, when we get home, I'll always fondly remember the travel posters!"

"I GAVE AT THE OFFICE!"

August 5, 1974

The original artwork for the next two months of comics has captions written in Fred's own handwriting.

August 6, 1974

"I KNOW YOU'RE A CAMERA NUT, DOC. BUT AT $75.00 A CRACK..."

August 7, 1974

"CLOSED GENERATION GAP TODAY... THE KID AND I
TALKED FOR THREE MINUTES, TEN SECONDS!"

August 8, 1974

"THEY SAY YOU WORRY MORE ABOUT GIRLS ___
BUT THE WAY HE'S DRESSED..."

August 9, 1974

August 10, 1974

August 12, 1974

August 13, 1974

"IT'S JUST NOT THE SAME OL' MEN'S BAR AND GRILL ANYMORE!"

August 14, 1974

Court rulings have prevented men's clubs from excluding women, though (surprisingly) a few clubs like this still exist.

August 15, 1974

"SURE IT'S HOT, BUT MAYBE YOU'LL LOSE A FEW POUNDS!"

274

"JUST ANOTHER BARBER SHOP NIGHTMARE!"

August 16, 1974

'I buy "Playboy" for the articles!' was a popular claim by men everywhere. Naked models aside, "Playboy" always included lifestyle and entertainment articles in every issue.

August 17, 1974

"I'M HOLDING OUT FOR BIG MONEY_HUGH HEFNER WANTS ME FOR HIS FASHION PAGES!"

August 19, 1974

"ANY MOMENT NOW THERE'S GOING TO BE EQUAL PAY AROUND HERE!"

Marshall McLuhan's catchphrase "The Medium is the Message" was first published in 1964 and is still taught in classrooms everywhere.

August 20, 1974

"IF 'THE MEDIUM IS THE MESSAGE,' WE'VE GOT A MOHAWK ON OUR HANDS!"

August 21, 1974

August 22, 1974

"HONESTLY, WE DON'T GET A LOT OF CALLS THESE DAYS FOR BULLDOG DRUMMOND!"

August 23, 1974

Bulldog Drummond is an adventurer whose exploits appeared in a series of fictional novels dating back to the 1920s.

August 24, 1974

"A TERRIFIC POLICY... IN CASE YOU EAT YOURSELF INTO A COMA BEFORE YOU'RE 65!"

August 26, 1974

Unisex bathrooms were a shocking concept in the 1970s and became the subject of a controversial debate during the near ratification of the Equal Rights Amendment.

August 27, 1974

August 28, 1974

"HE'S GOT NOTHING TO OFFER AND HE WANTS TO SHARE IT WITH US!"

August 29, 1974

"BLESS HIS LITTLE POINTED HEAD, THAT'S AN ORDINARY CIGARETTE HE'S SMOKING!"

August 30, 1974

August 31, 1974

September 2, 1974

"I BABIED THORNSBY THROUGH NICOTINE WITHDRAWAL, AND NOW HE GIVES UP POT!"

September 3, 1974

"AGE CATCHES UP WITH SOME OF US FASTER THAN OTHERS ... HE'S ONLY 27!"

September 4, 1974

"DON'T JUST STAND THERE GAPING_ TELL ME IF YOUR MOTHER'S STILL AWAKE!"

A Quonset hut is a nondescript prefabricated structure. The military used hundreds of thousands of these buildings during World War II.

September 5, 1974

"IT'D BE INSTANT NOSTALGIA_ON YOU, IT'D LOOK LIKE A W.W.II QUONSET HUT!"

September 6, 1974

"Y'KNOW, IF YOUR ULCERS WERE IN THE SAME SHAPE AS YOUR TICKER, I'D BE WORRIED!"

September 7, 1974

"CERTAINLY IT'S A CLASSIC — IT'S A 1925 PRETENTIOUS!"

September 9, 1974

Patina is a very clever name for Thornsby's elderly co-worker. Patina is the discoloration that forms on the surface of bronze and other metals due to age and oxidation.

"YES, OL' PATINA'S A NICE GUY, AND WISE BEYOND HIS YEARS!"

Thornsby paid tribute to all of the great bandleaders who influenced Fred during his boyhood years. Artie Shaw was a huge star during the 1930s and 1940s.

September 10, 1974

"IF THE NEWS UPSETS YOU, PROTEST! RUN OUT IN THE STREET AND BREAK ALL OF YOUR ARTIE SHAW RECORDS!"

September 11, 1974

"BOY ARE YOU LUCKY! THE DOC'S LATE SO I GET TO DO A CLEANING!"

September 12, 1974

"HOW'S THE BUDGET WORKING, HON?"

"YOU'VE LOVELY MANNERS, DEAR, BUT YOU JUST TIPPED YOUR HAT TO TWO TEEN-AGED BOYS!"

September 13, 1974

Fred celebrated his beloved Morgan sports car in numerous paintings and drawings, as well as hundreds of photographs. It was his favorite 'model.'

September 14, 1974

"YOU HAD TO ASK!"

September 16, 1974

The St. Louis Post-Dispatch refused to run 10 Thornsby comics during 1974. Apparently the X-rated movie poster for 'Lotsa Lust' was too racy for their comic page.

In 1914 Vice-President Thomas R. Marshall coined the phrase: "what this country needs is a really good five-cent cigar" (a quote that Fred enjoyed). Cheap cigars used to cost less than $1 during the 70s.

September 17, 1974

September 18, 1974

Fred's son Fred loved chemistry and even had a home laboratory in the basement (though not for the drug-related purposes that Tune-In had in this comic).

September 19, 1974

September 20, 1974

"HE MAY TAKE A DRINK NOW AND THEN, BUT THANK HEAVENS HE HAS NO OTHER VICES!"

September 21, 1974

"O.K. THESE LITTLE ENGLISH JOBS CAN TAKE ANY HILL, BUT CAN YOU GET IT DOWN?"

September 23, 1974

"THEY BEGAN AS SIT-UPS AND ENDED AS ROLL-OVERS!"

September 24, 1974

"BACK IN HIGH SCHOOL THERE WAS THIS BIG, DUMB BLONDE, AND NOW, WHENEVER HE HEARS THAT SONG..."

September 25, 1974

"PAYING YOU WHAT YOU'RE WORTH IS NO PROBLEM. WE'LL JUST TAKE IT OUT OF PETTY CASH!"

One of Fred's favorite quotes came from LBJ (President Johnson), who referred to Gerald Ford as someone who "played too much football with his helmet off."

September 26, 1974

"THE TUX HELPS, BUT YOU STILL LOOK LIKE YOU PLAYED A LOT OF FOOTBALL — WITHOUT A HELMET!"

September 27, 1974

" I'M SURE SHE NOTICED YOU. NOTICED YOUR PAUNCH, SQUINTY EYES, AND SHINY LITTLE HEAD! "

Austin High is frequently used in the Thornsby comics and was not a randomly chosen school. Fred was a jazz enthusiast who remembered 'The Austin High Gang' was a Chicago-based jazz group that gained fame in the 1920s.

September 28, 1974

SEPTEMBER SONG

"The Tailor was right! It <u>does</u> make me look 30 again!"

September 30, 1974

Fred's original handwritten caption was: "Now it's silly to try and look 30 again, but you must admit this vest does the trick!"

October 1, 1974

"Now that we've had a fiasco, are we too old to start a family?"

"If I have to listen to 'The Way We
Were' once more, I'll flip out!"

October 2, 1974

Barbra Streisand's "The Way We
Were" was the best-selling record
of 1974, ranked #1 on Billboard's
Year-End Hot 100 Singles list.

Note the framed picture of Fred
(in his trademark profile) on the
wall.

October 3, 1974

"Leave this house this minute or he'll
come over there and fall on you!"

"If that were hard rock they're check-
ing out, there'd be hope for them!"

October 4, 1974

President Ford played football at
the University of Michigan, but
Fred's favorite college football
team was Notre Dame. The
McLarens drove from Illinois to
Indiana to see a Notre Dame
game in the late 1960s.

October 5, 1974

"It's an old football injury - one
October day, when only Jerry Ford
and I could stop Notre Dame..."

"Where did we go wrong? That question
is about 20 years too late!"

October 7, 1974

October 8, 1974

"Sure she answered you.
She said, 'No way'."

"Please stop referring to your father as 'World War II memorabilia'!"

October 9, 1974

Neat freak Fred was always on the watch for germs and contamination (even on the family's silverware), much to his wife Betty Lou's exasperation.

October 10, 1974

"When you eat in a strange place, and wherever you eat is a strange place, always clean the silverware!"

October 11, 1974

"Well, if you like horror pictures, you'll love your X-rays!"

October 12, 1974

"'Hero' here can't get up, doc! Break it to him gently about his being cut from the team!"

"2-track, 4-track, railroad track! We were happy with a windup Victrola!"

October 14, 1974

The now obsolete 8-Track tape was a popular alternative to vinyl from the mid-1960s to early 1980s.

October 15, 1974

"Great Scot, Blanch! - You have lost weight!"

"He's everything we ever hoped for – industrious, gracious, impeccably attired..."

October 16, 1974

Fred begrudgingly accepted bi-focal and tri-focal glasses in his everyday life as he aged. His detailed artwork required vision as perfect as possible.

October 17, 1974

"Tri-focals aren't really noticeable, it's just that you seem to be behind a set of Venetian blinds!"

October 18, 1974

"It's just their way of telling you that Main St. has changed, dear!"

October 19, 1974

"Sure it's a toy, but he says it makes up for that electric train he never got!"

October 21, 1974

"Good morning! It's another
beautiful Monday!"

October 22, 1974

"Tell him he looks nice. He's dressed
up to be best man at a wedding!"

"They've never been able to communicate,
but at least they try!"

October 23, 1974

The five cent bottle of Coca-Cola lasted (amazingly) for over 70 years from the mid-1880s to the late 1950s.

October 24, 1974

"Oh, he's not so old, but he's the only one I know who remembers the 5¢ Coke."

October 25, 1974

"When I went to college, all I had was $20 and a dictionary!"

October 26, 1974

"Well, you see, he never speaks to anyone after starting a new diet!"

"You promised me a rose garden!"

October 28, 1974

Lynn Anderson's hit version of "(I Never Promised You a) Rose Garden" was released in 1970 and has become a country/pop standard.

President Ford's infamous pardoning of President Nixon for any crimes he might have committed against the United States occurred on September 8, 1974.

October 29, 1974

"If I'm reading the smoke signals right, the Jerry Ford honeymoon has gone into phase II."

"Ah...away from civilization at last!"

October 30, 1974

The McLaren family never went camping. Even with the rise of luxury motorhomes, the comforts of home were highly preferred.

October 31, 1974

"Beware of creeps bearing gifts!"

November 1, 1974

"Give up pot, study hard and join the establishment -- to end up looking like him?"

Fred always preferred the medium of radio over television. He listened to transistor radios throughout his entire life, including his retired years.

November 2, 1974

"He had a great future...34 years ago."

November 4, 1974

"Your first mistake was sending
him to his room!"

November 5, 1974

"He thought a unisex cut would
make him more masculine!"

November 6, 1974

Fred's son Tom never missed an Ann-Margret TV special during the 1970s, when headliner variety programs were still very popular.

"It's called 'open marriage'. I know where he is every minute, but I let him watch Ann-Margret."

Why do dentists and hygienists always ask questions when your mouth is filled with dental tools?

November 7, 1974

"He must agree with me. He hasn't said a word since he came in!"

"Next time, bury those old
copies of 'Penthouse'!"

November 8, 1974

November 9, 1974

"I'm glad you quit, son. I figure
anyone who can't get along without
cigarettes has got a problem!"

November 11, 1974

"It just dawned on me why you've never had an obscene phone call!"

November 12, 1974

"Hand over my guitar, pop. This place needs some acid rock this morning!"

November 13, 1974

"What's the matter with you? You
haven't complained about my
cigars all evening!"

See the sign for Rt. 22 on the left.
Illinois Route 22 is a highway in
northeastern Illinois and one of
the many roads where Fred would
drive his Morgan.

November 14, 1974

"Gee, it's nice to see our highway
tax dollars at work again!"

November 15, 1974

After a hard day at the office in Chicago, Fred would always take a short nap before dinner.

"To think there was a time when I called him 'tiger'!"

November 16, 1974

"It was Michigan and Missouri tied at 72 with a minute to go when I gave it my famous hook shot!"

November 18, 1974

"He's the only person I know who
hates airplanes and loves flying!"

November 19, 1974

"Lousy teeth, but check those reflexes!"

November 20, 1974

Dial-A type phone calls offered all kinds of entertainment during the prime 1970s years of rotary and push-button phones.

"Either you stick with your diet or no more 'dial-nostalgia'!"

November 21, 1974

"Aw, c'mon, dear -- you're always telling me, 'think positive'!"

November 22, 1974

"The doc said it's hopeless -- I'm a white, Anglo-Saxon Protestant with post nasal drip!"

November 23, 1974

"I know, hon. We all see what we want to see."

November 25, 1974

"I do belong to weight watchers. Every week I watch it go up 2 pounds!"

November 26, 1974

"If you see a fat little man with big glasses in here, call this number!"

"You win! You win! I'll give up rock if you'll stop singing 'Jeannie with the light brown hair'!"

November 27, 1974

"Jeanie with the Light Brown Hair" was a parlor song from the 1800s, with an opening line immortalized in the 1965-1970 TV series "I Dream of Jeannie" starring Barbara Eden.

November 28, 1974

"I know what I'm thankful for -- a perfectly logical excuse to put away all these calories!"

November 29, 1974

Denim expanded from its prior use as a work clothes standard to an everyday fashion staple during the 70s.

"Sure, kids wear denim. Car seats, luggage, boots, even TV sets wear it. But you're not leaving the house!"

Though its popularity has waned since the first half of the twentieth century, milk flavoring product Ovaltine has survived for more than one hundred years.

November 30, 1974

"Ovaltine? You've carried this 'golden days of yesteryear' campaign too far!"

December 2, 1974

"If corrective lenses are used, (Box C), subtract birth date from time of last traffic violation (Box 3-T), see 2E..."

December 3, 1974

"They found some old letters in the attic, and, next thing I knew, out came all the Harry James records!"

December 4, 1974

"Why not wait 'till <u>he's</u> 45 and
ask for another poster!"

Fred's favorite Christmas book
was Charles Dickens' "A
Christmas Carol." The only movie
adaptation of Scrooge's story
which he liked was the 1951 film
starring Alastair Sim.

December 5, 1974

"Let's just go home, light a fire
and re-read 'A Christmas Carol'."

December 6, 1974

"Appendix?! We'll never find it!"

December 7, 1974

"You'd get along better if you'd stop calling him 'Lenny Limpwrist'!"

December 9, 1974

"He keeps talking about retirement,
but I think it'll come as a giant
anticlimax!"

December 10, 1974

"Would I lie to you? I often
ask myself how I won the hand
of the sexiest girl in town!"

December 11, 1974

"And pressing down the homestretch,
the famous long-distance jogger..."

December 12, 1974

"Here's that nostalgia freak -- get
out the 'Remember 1939' sign!"

"At these prices, I'll have to cut you down to five square meals a day!"

December 13, 1974

December 14, 1974

"That's a nice outfit. I assume your 'care' package finally arrived!"

December 16, 1974

"It's now 10 o'clock and it's still Monday morning!"

December 17, 1974

"Brace yourself: you'll grow bald, gain weight and have problems relating to young people."

"With that stuff he smokes, he still has 'visions of sugarplums' dancing in his head!"

December 18, 1974

"While visions of sugar-plums danced in their heads" is a famous line from Clement C. Moore's poem "'Twas the Night Before Christmas." It was a McLaren family tradition to read this poem out loud on Christmas Eve.

December 19, 1974

"These days if you're well-groomed, the cute ones just flock around!"

"Now that you've tucked it in,
don't forget the aspirin!"

December 20, 1974

During the cold Midwest winter months, Fred would indeed go into the garage and place a blanket over the engine of his Morgan sports car to "keep it warm."

Fred enjoyed ice skating, but he never played hockey. Hickory Creek behind the family home in New Lenox would freeze over during the winter months, giving the McLarens their own private skating rink.

December 21, 1974

"Sure you can play -- just sit
in front of the goal!"

December 23, 1974

"I'm all set: a pot pipe for gramps, a leather purse for dad and hip huggers for mom!"

The original art for this comic is framed and hanging proudly in the home of Fred's son Tom and daughter-in-law Mary. It is a happy memory of McLaren Christmas past.

December 24, 1974

"Now that the shopping's done, and everything mailed, and the tree decorated, we can sit back and remember our bank account!"

"Happy, happy Christmas... that can recall
to the old man the pleasures of his youth..."
- *Charles Dickens, The Pickwick Papers.*

December 25, 1974

The Christmas chapter of Charles Dickens' "The Pickwick Papers" was on Fred's very short list of holiday favorites.

December 26, 1974

"It's O.K., hon. Once a pacesetter,
always a pacesetter!"

December 27, 1974

"I was being nice: I told my chick the ol' man was 'real heavy'!"

December 28, 1974

"Vacation? Looks like he's been on vacation since school started!"

December 30, 1974

"I've heard of padded timesheets and padded expense accounts, but this is ridiculous!"

December 31, 1974

"Y'see, Blanch. You have to <u>prepare</u> for New Year's Eve!"

January 1, 1975

"Tell him! Tell him you're only putting him on!"

January 2, 1975

"This is a recording - Congratulations! You just made weakling-of-the-week!"

January 3, 1975

"Face it, not everyone loves
to play trivia-time!"

January 4, 1975

"Burt Reynolds will be
with you in a moment!"

January 6, 1975

"14 years of music lessons gave him a fine, sensitive taste... for pure noise!"

January 7, 1975

"The main thing about a college roommate is having someone you can <u>relate</u> to!"

"Oh, it's amazing! Now you look just like an aviator!"

January 8, 1975

Long before Tom Cruise and "Top Gun," aviator glasses had a resurgence of popularity in the 70s. Fred wore this eyeglass style for many years.

January 9, 1975

"He's out of town, so I'll lay a little acid rock on ya!"

January 10, 1975

"Yes, she is... but she needed the job.
She's all alone, except for her mother,
who's sick..."

Looking less like a hippie, Tune-In
gets a haircut for the remainder
of Thornsby's run.

January 11, 1975

"Cheer up! If I flunk out, you'll
have me back home all year!"

January 13, 1975

"I'll show these at the medical convention. I've always wanted to be a comedian!"

"The Sensuous Woman" and "The Sensuous Man" were trendy best-selling books that helped ignite the sexual revolution.

January 14, 1975

"'The Sensuous Collector' just doesn't have the right ring to it!"

"I liked him, too, when I was a kid, but I got over it!"

January 15, 1975

It's much more acceptable to be a 'nerd' in today's world, than it was in 1975.

January 16, 1975

"Let's be glad it's a molar. Can you imagine filling a cavity like that?"

January 17, 1975

"Come along, dear. Remember,
you're driving!"

January 18, 1975

"Next time we lend 'the nice old guy'
your sled!"

January 20, 1975

"Since you're delivering last year's mail, how 'bout a cup of last year's coffee?"

Fred did own a raggedy brown sweater, full of holes and dangling loose threads, which he kept until it literally fell apart.

January 21, 1975

"I know you're attached to your old school sweater, hon, but nothing lasts forever!"

January 22, 1975

"First he lost faith in Nixon, then Ford and then the economy. But his fantasies are still going strong!"

January 23, 1975

"The doc did say it would take awhile to get used to tri-focals, hon!"

January 24, 1975

"I give up! Here, you can
have back your cigarettes!"

January 25, 1975

"It may have been 'made for you', but
you weren't made for it!"

"By the way, his opinions do not
necessarily reflect those of
of this network!"

January 27, 1975

Alice Cooper was born Vincent
Damon Furnier. The name
originally referred to the Alice
Cooper band, but became
synonymous with the 'shock rock'
frontman.

January 28, 1975

"If we can convince him that Alice
Cooper is a boy, we can convince
him of anything!"

"He went from Eagle Scout to flower child to ecology expert in less than one year!"

January 29, 1975

January 30, 1975

"It's just a formality."

January 31, 1975

The rich doctor's license plate is 60606, which was the zip code for Thornsby's Chicago-based newspaper syndicate.

"The recession has hit him hard. That's last year's Mercedes!"

February 1, 1975

"Even if we could afford it, with our luck it'd be recalled before delivery!"

February 3, 1975

Sherlock Holmes was another one of Fred's literary favorites. "The Complete Sherlock Holmes" by Sir Arthur Conan Doyle was gifted to his son Tom for Christmas 1980.

"Well, to begin with, Sherlock Holmes was tall, thin and ..."

February 4, 1975

"Look sharp! One wrong turn and we end up in Mexico City!"

February 5, 1975

"Of course I can recommend a diet. I take it you like bread and water?"

February 6, 1975

"I know he's trying hard to give up tobacco, but remember, he was fifteen before we got him off his pacifier!"

February 7, 1975

The Carpenters remain one of pop music history's most successful duos. Karen Carpenter's tragic death in 1983 at the age of 32 cut their career short.

"What gap? I merely said that I like the carpenters, too. They're one of the stongest trade unions around!"

February 8, 1975

"But you are liberated! I did the Saturday dishes three weeks ago all by myself!"

"Now stop hiding from Monday
and eat your breakfast!"

February 10, 1975

During 1973-1974, Arab members of OPEC (Organization of the Petroleum Exporting Countries) imposed an embargo against the United States, sparking the nation's shocking oil crisis.

February 11, 1975

"Maybe if we change our politics,
the Arabs will invest in our '75
budget plan!"

"I know you want a complete set of
National Geographic, but there's
been a lot of talk!"

February 12, 1975

One man's trash is another man's treasure. Fred loved used bookstores which, against all odds, still exist in small numbers throughout the US. Fred's son Tom had his first job as a teenager at a used bookstore named City Lights Bookshop in London, Ontario.

February 13, 1975

"If you're lucky, maybe she could go
for a bald-headed, middle-aged sexist!"

February 14, 1975

"Your offer of six free dancing lessons is certainly generous, but I just can't use 'em. You see, I'm a professional!"

The Midwest is known for weather extremes. Fred's Morgan sports car was forced to hibernate in the garage for the majority of the year.

Thornsby's garage is an exact duplicate of the family's garage in New Lenox, Illinois.

February 15, 1975

"Sure, I think a $5000 car is a fine investment. Especially since you can only drive it three months each year!"

February 17, 1975

"Just because I gave you flowers for Valentine's Day doesn't mean you have to dress up every morning!"

February 18, 1975

"Prices will go up and you'll be out of work. But take heart, Washington will send you a 37¢ refund!"

"I like to identify with movies, too, and 'Chinatown' was a winner. But if you go to the office like that..."

February 19, 1975

"Chinatown" paid homage to the Golden Age of Hollywood and was one of Fred's favorite 1970s films. The movie was set in 1937 and Thornsby is holding a picture of FDR (President Roosevelt), who served as President from 1933 to 1945.

February 20, 1975

"High prices or not - the rest of us get hungry, too!"

"'Warning: this magazine is hazardous to the health of old men with high blood pressure'!"

February 21, 1975

An unnamed college-aged daughter was added to the Thornsby family for the remainder of the comic's run.

February 22, 1975

February 24, 1975

"I TOLD you! No phone calls for him on Monday mornings 'til after coffee!"

February 25, 1975

"I'm keeping him on the straight and narrow, but it's a full-time job!"

February 26, 1975

"You <u>know</u> I understand nostalgia.
But for the late 60's?"

February 27, 1975

"I'm not saying he's a bore, but
he never uses one word where
seven or eight will do!"

February 28, 1975

"It's hard to tell. It could be
vandals, or it might be our
'Urban Progress Society'."

March 1, 1975

"Yes, dear. You're holding up much
better than the old school sweater."

March 3, 1975

"What is it this morning...a toothache or another fad diet?"

March 4, 1975

"Don't talk about your grades until he's been fed and watered!"

March 5, 1975

"I'm not sure you're self-destructive, but I AM sure I don't want to be around if it ever happens!"

March 6, 1975

"Okay...I take our budget seriously, you take it seriously - but an annual report for the neighbors?"

March 7, 1975

"If you had to dress up for a date, you might have at least warned him!"

Look for the self-portrait of Fred on the wall with the initials FM in the lower right corner.

March 8, 1975

"Don't tell me, it's a train! No, it's a duck! No, it's...maybe you'd better tell me!"

March 10, 1975

"We had a rock group at church yesterday, but he's beginning to unwind!"

March 11, 1975

"...and this is my husband, who believes pollution, like charity, begins at home!"

"Don't weaken! You've made it passed
Hamburger Heaven and Pancake Paradise.
One more donut shop and you're home!"

March 12, 1975

Fred's favorite resting spot was always the local donut shop. From Tim Hortons to Dunkin' Donuts, Fred loved to relax with a cup of coffee and a donut.

The Detroit Free Press edited out 'one more donut shop and you're home!,' due to space limitations.

Fred's son Tom is grateful to have inherited and saved many of his father's collectibles. It is the family's heritage, indeed.

March 13, 1975

"It's not a junk room; it's called
'Our Heritage'!"

March 14, 1975

"I told him we were 'into yoga' and he runs straight to the fridge to see what's missing!"

March 15, 1975

"That's no good. Just put the prices on each row. That'll scare anything!"

March 17, 1975

"All right, all right! You've got the raise!"

March 18, 1975

"O.K., we'll flip to see who answers it!"

March 19, 1975

"Here comes a real weirdo!"

March 20, 1975

"But sir, there's no way we can give a rebate on a 1949 Morgan!"

March 21, 1975

"I think he's doin' better than 55 mph!"

March 22, 1975

"And then you said, 'A recession will always bring prices down'!"

March 24, 1975

March 25, 1975

"Why not start with something simple --
like a high-wire act?"

March 26, 1975

Martial arts is a popular form of
self-improvement, but breaking is
a technique that the everyman
rarely masters.

March 27, 1975

"Well, you'll never see that one again!"

"He'll never adjust to suburbia: every night he looks for neon signs!"

March 28, 1975

Although Fred lived in a variety of cities from small town suburbia to the Near North Side of Chicago, he preferred the hustle and bustle of the big city for the final three decades of his life.

March 29, 1975

"I know we should all save on fuel, but why must you go to extremes?"

March 31, 1975

"Well, y'know -- it's a living!"

April 1, 1975

"My own daughter!"

"Know something? I've finally had it with nostalgia!"

April 2, 1975

Double-digit inflation and other socioeconomic factors wreaked havoc on the fluctuating value of the US dollar in the 1970s.

April 3, 1975

"Now, repeat after me: a dollar is a quarter, a quarter is a dime, a dime is a . . ."

"Let's compromise -- stay out of the fridge for one night and I'll double your allowance!"

April 4, 1975

April 5, 1975

"His Saturday mornings are just one ego trip after another."

April 7, 1975

"Someday this will all be yours!"

Fred collected comic books throughout his life, but in later years it was more for the appreciation of a particular artist than the storylines.

April 8, 1975

"Man, the adult section is on the other side of the store!"

April 9, 1975

"There's one on every block who insists on being the first out each spring!"

April 10, 1975

"Remember -- dogs love a fat man."

"Maybe your diet's a success!"

"They love a bedtime story. But two hours of Howard Cosell?"

April 11, 1975

With his unique voice and style, Howard Cosell was the ultimate 'love him or hate him' radio and television sportscaster.

April 12, 1975

"If you really buy the lib bit, you don't need MY help!"

April 14, 1975

"Brace yourself. His music
has all the excitement of a
Gerald Ford speech!"

April 15, 1975

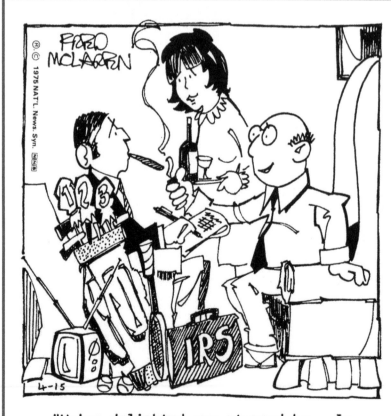

"We're delighted you stopped by. Is
there anything else we can get you?"

April 16, 1975

It was the norm back then that barber shops were men only, while beauty shops were women only.

"Mine's the one with the girlie magazine!"

April 17, 1975

"Don't be silly - no one would ever suspect you're a tourist!"

April 18, 1975

Fred's books were his treasured collectibles and he never embraced the concept of a digital book. He joined various hard copy book clubs during his lifetime.

"You know you're over the hill when you take a lifetime membership in the Nostalgia Book Club!"

Released in December 1974, "The Towering Inferno" was one of the most successful films of 1975 and is remembered as the greatest of the 1970s disaster films. Fred's son Tom had the movie poster on his bedroom wall.

April 19, 1975

"And now, the award for lowest grades in the class. And the winner is: 'The Towering Inferno'!"

April 21, 1975

"Nervous? A tax audit
could hardly make ME nervous!"

April 22, 1975

"Very funny."

"We all have our hang-ups, Dear!"

April 23, 1975

Fred had a 6 foot poster of scantily clad Warren magazine heroine "Vampirella" on his den wall. The artwork was by artist Jose Gonzalez.

April 24, 1975

"Maybe they're sick an' tired of 'Little Red Riding Hood'!"

April 25, 1975

"I have to give him credit: He brings
a lot of work home from the office!"

Look closely at the license plates
on the garage wall: 60451 was
the McLaren home's zip code in
New Lenox, Illinois; N6H 3H7 was
the McLaren home's zip code in
London, Ontario.

April 26, 1975

"Before you give 'it' a bath, the
forecast calls for rain, followed
by a dust storm!"

April 28, 1975

"Isn't it wonderful? After years of working and saving, we've got a place to call our own!"

April 29, 1975

"Just a trim?"

April 30, 1975

"Just what we need: Three sets of Encyclopedia Britannica!"

May 1, 1975

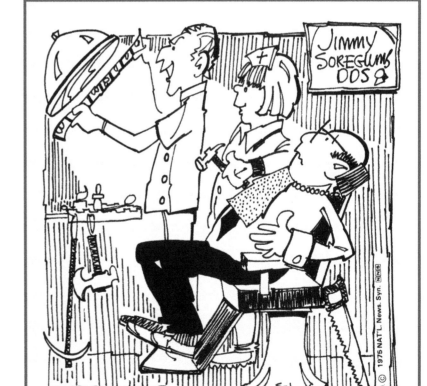

"Not too serious: First we'll remove the gums, and then...."

May 2, 1975

The McLaren family lived in the little town of New Lenox, Illinois (no skyscrapers there) until 1973. Subsequent moves to Ontario and then Michigan came with big business encroaching on small town suburbia.

"Suburbia's a lot of fun: at night you can walk around and count all the skyscrapers!"

May 3, 1975

"O.K., you didn't expect a scene like that. Now sit down!"

May 5, 1975

"It's not MY fault! We moved from the 12th to the 7th floor and she came with the furniture!"

May 6, 1975

"You ever answer the door in that rag and I'm seeing a lawyer the next day!"

"Who else would come in here and order a bowl of Wheaties?"

May 7, 1975

Fred preferred American food and never ate in an Asian restaurant. One of his all-time favorites was in downtown Chicago: the German restaurant Berghoff's, with its stylish setting and meat & potatoes menu.

Published from 1939 to 1955, "Startling Stories" was one of many pulp magazines which Fred loved and collected.

May 8, 1975

"I've always loved the classics -- I've got every issue of 'Startling Stories'!"

"Don't mention old time radio.
we'll be stuck for hours!"

May 9, 1975

Herb Alpert and the Tijuana Brass
was perhaps the only musical
group which the entire McLaren
family agreed upon. Everyone
had their own vinyl copy of the
classic album "Whipped Cream &
Other Delights."

May 10, 1975

"What problem? I only said
Herb Alpert couldn't carry Harry James
trumpet case!"

May 12, 1975

"It's wonderful. In 30 years I've paid $100,000 in taxes. Now I get $100 back!"

Fred's Morgan had a detachable folding roof (which was not very practical for rain or sleet days). The sound of rain on that roof is unmistakable.

May 13, 1975

"Oh, I just LOVE the sound of rain on the roof!"

May 14, 1975

"They DO something for you — you look like the only 50-year-old hippie around!"

May 15, 1975

"If you'll just stand still, I'll explain every-thing!"

"It's just that he's never heard "Onward Christian Soldiers' played that way!"

May 16, 1975

"Onward, Christian Soldiers" is a 19th century hymn that has endured through the centuries.

May 17, 1975

"No dear, you'll never lose the male mystique!"

"Around here Mondays are like that!"

"No, he hasn't turned aggressive . . . he's just getting ready to ride the subway!"

"He said he's giving up 'liberal parenthood'!"

May 21, 1975

Thornsby is throwing Tune-In's guitar on the outdoor grill. Like many Midwestern families in suburbia, the McLaren family barbecued outside during the summer months. One favorite was Fred's wife Betty Lou's shish kebab marinade.

The Great Society was a broad reform package launched by President Johnson in 1964-65.

The silent majority was a term first popularized by President Nixon in 1969.

May 22, 1975

"I joined the 'great society' and the 'silent majority' — so now I'm a big success!"

May 23, 1975

"It looks so natural no one would ever guess!"

May 24, 1975

"Sure you're old and fat and worn out. But you've got seniority!"

May 26, 1975

"I guess we're doing all right. It only takes 99 per cent of our income for food and rent!"

May 27, 1975

"We took special care of this — your husband said it was his best sweater!"

"He SAYS he was out photographing BIRDS!"

May 28, 1975

'Birds' was a British slang expression referring to women (and is now viewed as sexist by many women).

Recognize that face on the TV screen?

May 29, 1975

"Thank Heaven! The energy crisis strikes home!"

"We were for his 'Project Independence'. How do we stand on his 'Project Interdependence'?"

May 30, 1975

Project Independence (launched by Nixon in 1973) was a US program to make the country more energy self-sufficient. Project Interdependence (launched by Ford in 1974) was a global program that encouraged international cooperation to save our vital energy resources.

"Jack Armstrong, the All-American Boy" was a popular radio series from 1933 to 1951. Fred collected reel-to-reel tapes of these old shows.

May 31, 1975

"It's not a 'time warp' — he just ordered some Jack Armstrong tapes!"

"... and this is our efficiency expert..."

June 2, 1975

June 3, 1975

"Now I get it! We're supposed to buy a new car, but if we drive it, we're wasting gas and oil!"

June 4, 1975

"What luxury . . . to come home every night
to my pipe and slippers!"

June 5, 1975

"They loved your 900 Morgan-Four slides — but
it's 4:30 a.m.!"

June 6, 1975

"Just thought I'd get a bite before the next price rise!"

June 7, 1975

"We've had a rebate, a retread and a recall. Now I'd like a revenge!"

June 9, 1975

"Actually, only two of those have any fish in them!"

June 10, 1975

"He's had a terrible accident — he just fell off his shoes!"

June 11, 1975

"After he's had a hard day at the office, I hate to baby him!"

June 12, 1975

"Ready for your annual check-up?"

"I don't care if your mother is coming, you're not cleaning in here!"

June 13, 1975

Fred did not like his personal belongings to be touched by anyone.

Son Tom learned the 'mint condition' collector mentality from his father.

In 1975 President Ford passed into law the Metric Conversion Act, which recommended a voluntary conversion to the metric system. To date, metrication has never been officially adopted in the US.

June 14, 1975

"Think of it this way: the metric system makes everything EASY!"

"Man, I can understand that you NEED heels —
but that skinny tie's got to go!"

June 16, 1975

Styles come and go...the skinny ties popularized by the Beatles in the early 1960s would not return to fashion until the start of new wave in the late 1970s.

Long before video games, board games ruled leisure time in the 1970s. Some were aimed at an 'adults only' audience. The sexual undertones of the game Twister were obvious to all adults.

June 17, 1975

"Here's a winner, for two or more players —
'Cope Along with Ford'!"

June 18, 1975

"Once an overachiever, always an overachiever!"

With the fall of South Vietnam to communist North Vietnam on April 30, 1975, Ford and Kissinger were at the center of the US involvement controversy.

June 19, 1975

"Which is it today, Hon — 'Our Commitment' or 'Our Involvement'?"

"The only 'tummy TV' that'll fit him is a $600 Console!"

June 20, 1975

In the 1960s, Sony introduced the Tummy Television, a small portable TV that you could rest on your stomach while lying in bed.

June 21, 1975

"Yes, dear, it looks much better since it was washed and ironed."

"I don't care if you WERE a member of the 'Secret Squadron'! We're right on course!"

June 23, 1975

The "Captain Midnight" radio program featured a hero heading up the Secret Squadron, an aviation-oriented organization that defended America against its enemies.

June 24, 1975

"Oh, he just loves the grand entrance."

June 25, 1975

"O.K., your wife doesn't understand you. It's your fault. Will there be anything else?"

June 26, 1975

"Whoever told you clothes make the man was putting you on!"

"It just doesn't know HOW to play 'You Made Me Love You'!"

June 27, 1975

"You Made Me Love You (I Didn't Want to Do It)" is an American standard written in 1913 and recorded by a long list of popular singers including Al Jolson, Bing Crosby, Judy Garland, etc.

June 28, 1975

"What's wrong, dearheart — you look like you've lost your last credit card!"

"You've ruined my whole day."

June 30, 1975

Fred was never a morning person. He preferred to stay up all night and sleep until noon.

Ten degrees Celsius = 50 degrees Fahrenheit.

July 1, 1975

"Hon, ten degrees celsius doesn't mean it's freezing outside."

July 2, 1975

"Yes Mother, he's alive and well and living in a hovel!"

Thornsby's daughter (like many young adults in the 60s and 70s) loved vintage bohemian and retro clothing.

July 3, 1975

"It must be an expensive outfit — it looks pretty worn out!"

July 4, 1975

"We've x-rayed every angle, and after serious consideration, the left-front side is the funniest!"

July 5, 1975

"I can understand why you young fellows always go for racy, little sports cars!"

"Why aren't they happy? Fewer auto sales means just that many fewer recalls!"

July 7, 1975

Food City was a Canadian supermarket chain (which closed in the 1990s). Fred's wife Betty Lou shopped regularly at one located near their home in London, Ontario.

July 8, 1975

"O.K., they're making 'em smaller. How are you at high jump?"

"You'll never amount to anything if you don't learn to spend your spare time productively!"

July 9, 1975

July 10, 1975

" . . . with two out and Smith on third, Thornsby homered to give us a 4-2 victory . . ."

July 11, 1975

"I'll be a little late, Hon — my Great Books program is running a little long!"

Bix Biederbecke is considered one of the most influential jazz musicians of the 1920s. He died in 1931 at the age of 28 and was the inspiration for the classic 1950 film "Young Man With a Horn."

July 12, 1975

"How can you relate to anything called 'Beiderbecke'? Sounds like a skin disease!"

July 14, 1975

"I talked him into giving it to the Salvation Army — but they sent it back!"

July 15, 1975

"This ol' Jack Armstrong ring doesn't fit anymore, either."

July 16, 1975

"I suffer. I sacrifice. But I do get a TV dinner, a Gunsmoke re-run and a nice, quiet house!"

July 17, 1975

"I'm going off my diet! Five more pounds and the girls at the office will never be able to concentrate on their work!"

" . . . Sentimentalist that I am, I must admit that our relationship is based on your ability to project warmth and understanding . . . "

July 18, 1975

Did your parents tell you to 'clean your plate, there are starving children all over the world'?

July 19, 1975

"I know millions are hungry — I'm one of them!"

July 21, 1975

"It's slightly superficial — but it goes with your decor!"

July 22, 1975

"It won the '500' — it went 500 yards from the showroom before falling apart."

July 23, 1975

Auto production by the Big Three (Ford, GM, and Chrysler) dropped in the 70s due to many factors, including competition from foreign automobile companies, rising oil prices, and manufacturing disasters (remember the Ford Pinto?).

" . . . Dial Nostalgia now brings you 1973 and the sounds of an auto plant in full production . . ."

Clyde McCoy was a jazz trumpeter best known for his 1930s theme song "Sugar Blues."

July 24, 1975

"One more chorus of 'Sugar Blues' and I'm packing it in to mother!"

July 25, 1975

"You're right! It's that insurance man again!"

July 26, 1975

"I should warn you, dear — 'Mr. Fixit' has trouble turning on the TV!"

July 28, 1975

Football's front four consists of two defensive ends and two defensive tackles.

"Of course he played for Notre Dame — he was the 'Front Four'!"

July 29, 1975

"Fine. Dial A Prayer. Dial Henny Youngman. But the Playmate of the Month taking a Shower . . .?"

"We know it's 'special and one-of-a-kind' . . .
and so is our bill!"

July 30, 1975

GM stock price dropped to a
shocking low of $11.68/share on
January 2, 1975.

July 31, 1975

"Listen to him when he talks money . . . he
pulled our Standard Oil stocks and put them
into G.M.!"

August 1, 1975

"Of course you're liberated — I lit the candles!"

August 2, 1975

"Well, Jolly Green Giant, the law of averages
works . . . six carrots survived spring planting!"

"Oh, brother, Waldo Pepper's going to the corner store for a coke!"

August 4, 1975

"The Great Waldo Pepper" is a 1975 movie starring Robert Redford, who looked dashing in his 1920s cap and scarf. This was Fred's favorite cap style for many years.

August 5, 1975

"Of course you can still wear a bikini — BUT NOT OUTDOORS!"

August 6, 1975

"There! You see? We can never discuss religion or politics — you're too emotional!"

August 7, 1975

"I suppose, after a few years, we all have to face a receding hairline!"

August 8, 1975

"Actually, the braless look is so old hat by now that no one pays the slightest attention."

August 9, 1975

"Today's his big day: he turned 50 and broke 90!"

"His zipper broke, so he got safety pins, stuck his finger, saw blood, felt faint and fell down the steps."

August 11, 1975

Fred did suffer from vasovagal syncope - which means he did faint at the sight of blood.

Televisions using cathode ray tube (CRT) technology are now almost obsolete. Low cost CRT models continue to be sold outside of the United States.

August 12, 1975

"He's just like an old TV set — every six months another tube burns out!"

August 13, 1975

Wayne King was an orchestra leader known as the 'Waltz King.' He had a successful radio career in the 30s and 40s.

"What kind of juke box is it that doesn't have Wayne King?"

August 14, 1975

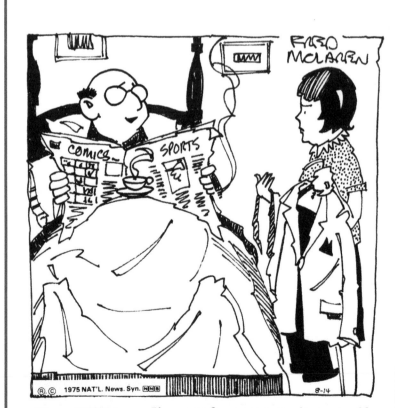

"I am NOT lazy. I'm merely programming myself for 'forced retirement'!"

"Let's face it, Blanch — once a sex object, always a sex object!"

August 15, 1975

"Two bites and a deep breath" was one of Fred's favorite phrases. Son Tom still uses it to this very day when describing disappointing portions of food.

August 16, 1975

"These receptions are fun . . . you're supposed to be full after two bites and a deep breath!"

431

August 18, 1975

"All right, I give in! Bad vibes are better than no vibes!"

August 19, 1975

"They put up with your sports car and your imitation of Harry James every night, but they might mention the yard . . . "

August 20, 1975

"The C.I.A. never rests!"

August 21, 1975

"What a rough day you've had — instant rice, instant potatoes, instant pudding, instant coffee — and you call it supper!"

August 22, 1975

"This is my husband. He likes cars!"

August 23, 1975

" . . . only an 'over-achiever' knows the value of deactivating after a hard day's work . . . "

August 25, 1975

"How can you buy a horoscope that says you'll meet a millionaire who's 'slim, blonde and your own age'?"

August 26, 1975

"I didn't say you had bad breath — but you ARE overdue for a cleaning!"

"Who needs TV? I've got my very own soap opera!"

August 27, 1975

Fred's son Tom described their family's life one day and his words became this caption. Fred kindly credited him in the artwork (see text on lower left side).

August 28, 1975

"You can tell this is unspoiled territory. I've only seen 144 beer cans today!"

August 29, 1975

"Now admit it — I never mention your weight problem — excuse me there's the phone"

August 30, 1975

"Now don't raise your voice — we must set an example for the children!"

September 1, 1975

"Maybe they are lovebirds . . . but to me he looks more like a Bald Eagle."

"Esquire" is still the longest-running American men's magazine, dating back to its first publication in 1933.

September 2, 1975

"Don't tear your hair out — they're only a bunch of old Esquires!"

September 3, 1975

One dollar per gallon was high (!) in 1975.

"Oh, I don't mind the idea of a dollar a gallon — but 5 miles to the gallon really bugs me!"

September 4, 1975

"What happens if we light ours five minutes before the rest of them?"

September 5, 1975

"But I want you to TRY and watch the 10 o'clock news WITHOUT getting upset!"

September 6, 1975

"Keep a straight face when he tells you it's his pride and joy!"

September 8, 1975

"He likes to keep busy . . . collecting stamps, watching TV, gaining weight . . . "

September 9, 1975

"You're not second place in my life — fourth, maybe . . . "

"There must be fewer girlie magazines on the market — I've got 20 cents left!"

September 10, 1975

Going to the newsstand to buy newspapers, magazines, and comic books was a routine for Fred and son Tom. Most print publications were still going strong during the 70s.

September 11, 1975

"I'm not saying he's a hypochondriac — but the last time I caught a cold HE checked into a hotel!"

September 12, 1975

"Do you suppose anyone's ever heard of a seventh mortgage?"

September 13, 1975

"Oh, come on now — nobody likes a quitter!"

September 15, 1975

"Sure it's hot — but 11 ice cream cones in a row will stop anyone."

September 16, 1975

"Pills have no effect and he won't stay on a diet. Now maybe a gigantic band-aid . . . "

September 17, 1975

"This may or may not be anti-feminist, but it's called 'Playbroad'!"

September 18, 1975

"I knew he had problems — but did you ever see stretch marks on teeth!?"

September 19, 1975

"Great Scott, Blanch! You've lost so much weight, y' look like a hatrack!"

September 20, 1975

"I'm one short of my quota tonight — but here comes Thornsby!"

"No way Joe Cool's gonna fall for a hair tonic commercial like that!"

September 22, 1975

'Joe Cool' is a nod to one of Snoopy's alter-egos in the popular newspaper comic strip "Peanuts" by Charles Schulz.

September 23, 1975

"Nothing serious . . . probably just trying to attract our attention."

"Bringing work home from the office, I see!"

September 24, 1975

"Down by the Old Mill Stream" was written by Tell Taylor in 1908. Popularized by many barbershop quartets, the song became a pop culture classic.

September 25, 1975

" . . . and then I wrote: 'Down by the Ol' Mill Stream'!"

448

September 26, 1975

"It MUST be sexy.   He's enjoying it."

The End.

September 27, 1975

The final published cartoon. September 27, 1975.

PUBLICATIONS (partial list)

	Newspaper	Start of Run
ST. LOUIS POST-DISPATCH	St. Louis Post-Dispatch (Missouri)	April 1973
Boston Herald American	Boston Herald American (Massachusetts)	April 1973
Star-Herald	Scottsbluff Star-Herald (Nebraska)	April 1973
THE POST-STANDARD	Syracuse Post Standard (New York)	May 1973
THE ANN ARBOR NEWS	Ann Arbor News (Michigan)	May 1973
Daily Press	Newport News Daily Press (Virginia)	May 1973
THE SUN	Baltimore Sun (Maryland)	June 1973
Detroit Free Press	Detroit Free Press (Michigan)	June 1973
The Charlotte Observer	Charlotte Observer (North Carolina)	July 1973
Chicago Daily News	Chicago Daily News (Illinois)	March 1974
The Evening Bulletin	Philadelphia Bulletin (Pennsylvania)	April 1974
Lincoln Evening Journal	Lincoln Evening Journal/Journal Star (Nebraska)	June 1974
The Tampa Times	Tampa Times (Florida)	November 1974

Fred McLaren self-portrait watercolor painting. 1980s.

Chapter 3

Thornsby: Unpublished Cartoons

Like deleted scenes from movies and previously unreleased tracks from music albums, the unpublished Thornsby cartoons are interesting and curious treasures to cherish. Regrettably, Fred is no longer with us to provide the background details to outstanding Thornsby questions. Nonetheless, these remaining comics provide a glimpse of Fred's creative process before, during, and after Thornsby's newspaper run.

As our book journey draws to a close, enjoy four never-before-seen comics.

The only four-panel strip known to still exist. The initial pitch deck references the original concept as panels and strips, so the strips were likely for a proposed Sunday newspaper version.

"WHERE'S THE GUY WHO INVENTED 'THE PILL' NOW THAT WE NEED HIM?"

A cartoon found as an original drawing. Note the question mark in the upper right margin. The reference to 'The Pill' was perhaps too controversial, so either Fred rejected this idea or the syndicate blocked publication.

A cartoon located on a proof sheet and unpublished for reasons unknown. It was likely held in reserve, in case a problem arose with another cartoon and a substitution was needed at the last minute.

"Man, you must have a wild money belt in there!"

"IT'S SIMPLE REAGANOMICS: I CUT YOUR ALLOWANCE 50%, DECLARE A DEFICIT, AND YOU'RE AHEAD 30%!"

A cartoon discovered as an original drawing. Fred contemplated a Thornsby revival in the early 1980s. This could have been the start of a whole new era. This is the last Thornsby ever created.

THE END

For more information and updates on Thornsby, see:

Facebook.com/thornsbybyfredmclaren

Instagram @thornsbybyfredmclaren

Twitter @thornsbymclaren

Acknowledgments

Thank you to Fred's family and friends, who have kept the flame alive and supported the memory of Thornsby to this very day. Special thanks to those who have saved and sent mementos of Fred's career to us through the years, including: David and Sharon McLaren, Nina and Kim Kaiser, Fred McLaren, Nicole McLaren, Chris Ledbetter, Bill Foster, and Tom Claggett. Apologies to those we may have inadvertently left out.

Fred presents granddaughter Nicole with a Thornsby original cartoon.
Chicago, Illinois. October 18, 2010.

Fred McLaren posing with framed Thornsby originals on the wall of Tom and Mary's home. Los Angeles, California. December 25, 2005.

About the Authors

An accomplished actor and published author, Tom McLaren started his adult life as a corporate finance executive at Warner Bros. and Twentieth Century Fox. In 2012 he made a mid-life career change and began acting in film, television, and commercials. Major credits include "Lost in Space" (Netflix TV series) & the feature films "Expelled" (Awesomeness), "Exorcism of Molly Hartley" (Fox) and "Santa's Little Helper" (Fox/WWE). He co-authored "Styling the Stars: Lost Treasures from the Twentieth Century Fox Archive," published by Insight Editions in both hardcover and softcover books. Currently, Tom is Co-Head of Next Chapter Entertainment's Production and Publishing divisions. He holds a BBA from the University of Michigan and an MBA from Wayne State University.

tom-mclaren.com
Facebook.com/tommclarenpage
Instagram and Twitter @tommclaren1

A career long Studio executive in Hollywood, Mary McLaren served as Chief Operating Officer, International Theatrical and Worldwide Home Entertainment, at Twentieth Century Fox for more than a decade. Currently, she is the CEO of Next Chapter Entertainment LLC, overseeing the Production, Publishing and Talent Mgmt. divisions. Recognized in the top half of "The Hollywood Reporter"' Power 100 Women in Entertainment list for multiple years, Mary is an active member of the Academy of Motion Picture Arts & Sciences and the Television Academy, as well as a mentor for rising talent across the major Studios' production & distribution divisions and for the Academy Gold program. She holds a BBA from the University of Michigan and an MBA from Wayne State University.

nextchapterent.com
Facebook.com/nextchapterentertainment
Instagram @nextchapterentertainment Twitter @nextchaptent

Tom and Mary live in Los Angeles with their two cats Cleo and Amber.

Lightning Source UK Ltd.
Milton Keynes UK
UKHW050311060321
379846UK00002B/89